IMITATE THEIR FAITH

This book is the property of

Kevin Wallace

April 2013 Printing

This publication is not for sale. It is provided as part of a worldwide Bible educational work
supported by voluntary donations.

Unless otherwise indicated, Scripture quotations are from the modern-language
New World Translation of the Holy Scriptures—With References.

Imitate Their Faith
English (*ia*-E)

Made in Germany
Druck und Verlag: Wachtturm-Gesellschaft, Selters/Taunus

To Our Dear Brothers and Sisters:

In its very first issue, January 1, 2008, the public edition of *The Watchtower* introduced us to a fascinating new series of articles entitled "Imitate Their Faith." Since then, a new article in that series has been published every three months, much to our delight!

What has been the response to the series? After she finished reading the article on Martha, one reader wrote: "I laughed when I read it because I'm just like her—always desiring to be a good hostess and to be busy but sometimes forgetful of the need to pause and enjoy association with the friends." A teenager drew this interesting conclusion from the story of Esther: "I could relate to the fact that we can be obsessed with clothes and the latest fashions. We should be well-groomed; yet, we don't want to go overboard." She added: "Jehovah cares about who we are inside." And an article featuring the apostle Peter elicited this enthusiastic reaction from a Christian sister: "You pulled me lock, stock, and barrel into the account. It came to life! I used my senses to feel what the passages only alluded to."

These readers—and countless others who have written to express their appreciation for the series—confirm what the apostle Paul wrote long ago: "All the things that were written aforetime were written for our instruction." (Rom. 15:4) Yes, Jehovah had these narratives included in the Bible in order to teach us valuable lessons. All of us, no matter how many years we have known the truth, can learn from them.

We warmly encourage you to read this book as soon as possible. Include it as part of your Family Worship program—the children will love it! When the congregation studies the material during the Congregation Bible Study, do not miss a single week! Take your time; read it slowly. Use your imagination; get your senses involved. Try to feel what those Bible characters felt, to see what they saw. Compare how they reacted in a given situation with the way you would likely have responded.

It gives us great pleasure to share this publication with you. May it prove to be a blessing to you and your family. With much love and every good wish,

Governing Body of Jehovah's Witnesses

IMITATE THEIR FAITH

Introduction

"Be imitators of those who through faith and patience inherit the promises."
—HEBREWS 6:12.

"HE SPEAKS about Bible characters as if they were old friends of his." After listening to a discourse by an elderly traveling overseer, a Christian woman made that observation. And rightly so, for the brother had spent decades studying God's Word and teaching from it—so much so that the Bible's men and women of faith did, indeed, seem like old friends whom he had known all his life.

2 Would not many of those Bible characters make wonderful friends? Are they that real to you? Imagine what it would be like to walk and talk with them, to spend time getting to know such men and women as Noah, Abraham, Ruth, Elijah, and Esther. Think of the influence they might have on your life—the precious words of advice and encouragement they might offer!—*Read Proverbs 13:20.*

3 Of course, at the time of the "resurrection of . . . the righteous," that kind of rewarding relationship will be fully possible.

(Acts 24:15) However, even right now we can benefit from learning about the Bible's men and women of faith. How? The apostle Paul offers this practical answer: "Be imitators of those who through faith and patience inherit the promises." (Heb. 6:12) As we embark on a study of the subject of men and women of faith, let us consider a few questions that Paul's words bring to mind: Just what is faith, and why do we need it? How can we imitate faithful people of old?

Faith—What It Is and Why We Need It

4 Faith is an appealing quality, one that all the men and women we will study about in this publication valued highly. Many people today tend to undervalue faith, assuming that it means believing without any real proof or evidence. However, they are mistaken. Faith is not gullibility; it is not a mere feeling; it is more than belief. Gullibility is dangerous. A mere feeling may come and go, and even belief is insufficient when it comes to God, for "the demons believe and shudder."—Jas. 2:19.

1, 2. How did one traveling overseer evidently view faithful Bible characters, and why would such ones make wonderful friends?

3. (a) How can we benefit from learning about the Bible's men and women of faith? (b) What questions will we consider?

4. What do people tend to assume about faith, and why are they mistaken?

What is faith?   *read b4 q's.*

5 True faith towers over such things. Recall how the Bible defines it. (*Read Hebrews 11:1.*) Paul said that faith focuses on two kinds of things that we cannot see. One, it focuses on present realities that are "not beheld." Our physical eyes cannot see the realities in the spirit realm—such as Jehovah God, his Son, or the Kingdom that now rules in heaven. Two, faith focuses on "things hoped for"—events that have not yet happened. We cannot now see the new world that God's Kingdom will soon bring about. Does that mean, then, that our faith in such realities and the things we have hoped for is groundless?

6 Far from it! Paul explained that true faith is solidly grounded. When he called faith "the assured expectation," he used an expression that may also be rendered "title deed." Imagine that someone decided to give you a house. He might hand you the deed to the place and say, "Here is your new home." Of course, he does not mean that you will live on that piece of paper; he means that the document is so legally binding that for all practical purposes, it *is* the house itself. Similarly, the evidence for our

faith is so convincing, so strong, that it may be equated to our faith itself.

7 Thus, true faith involves well-founded confidence and unshakable conviction that is clearly focused on Jehovah God. Faith causes us to see him as our loving Father and to trust that all his promises are sure to come true. But genuine faith involves more. Like a living thing, it must be nourished to survive. It must be expressed in actions, or it will die.—Jas. 2:26. *faith w/oot works is dead.*

8 Why is faith so important? Paul provided a compelling answer. (*Read Hebrews 11:6.*) We can neither approach Jehovah nor please him unless we have faith. So faith is essential if we are to fulfill the highest, noblest purpose of any intelligent creature: to draw close to and glorify our heavenly Father, Jehovah.

9 Jehovah knows how much we need faith, so he provides us with examples to teach us how to build and show faith. He blesses the Christian congregation with examples of faithful men who take the lead. His Word says: "Imitate their faith." (Heb. 13:7) And he has given us more. Paul wrote about a "great . . . cloud of witnesses," men

---

5, 6. (a) Our faith focuses on what two kinds of unseen things? (b) How solidly grounded should our faith be? Illustrate.

7. What does true faith involve?
8. Why is faith so important?
9. How has Jehovah shown that he is aware of our need for faith?

and women of ancient times who left sterling examples of faith. (Heb. 12:1) Paul's list of faithful ones, recorded in Hebrews chapter 11, is by no means complete. The Bible's pages are rich with true stories about men and women, young and old, from all walks of life, who lived lives of faith and who have much to teach us in these faithless times.

How Can We Imitate the Faith of Others?

10 You cannot imitate a person unless you first observe him closely. As you read through this publication, you will notice that much research has been done to help you observe these men and women of faith. Why not follow suit and do additional research of your own? In your personal study, dig into the Bible with the research tools you have at hand. As you meditate on what you study, try to picture the setting and background of Bible accounts. Try to see the sights, hear the sounds, smell the aromas, so to speak. More important, try to discern the feelings of the people involved. As you empathize with those faithful men and women, they will become more real to you, more familiar—some may even come to seem like dear old friends.

11 When you truly come to know them, you will want to imitate them. For instance, imagine contemplating a new assignment. Through Jehovah's organization, you are invited to expand your ministry in some way. Perhaps you are asked to move to a territory where there is an urgent need for more preachers, or maybe you are invited to try some form of preaching that you find unfamiliar or uncomfortable. As you contemplate the assignment and pray about it, would it help to meditate on the example of Abram? He and Sarai were willing to forgo the comforts of Ur and were richly blessed as a result. As you follow in their footsteps, you will surely feel that you now know them better than ever before.

12 Similarly, what if someone close to you were to treat you spitefully and you felt discouraged—even felt tempted to stay home from the meetings? If you contemplated Hannah's example and the way she rose above Peninnah's spitefulness, it would help you to make the right decision—and it might make Hannah seem more like a dear friend too. Likewise, if you are discouraged by feelings of worthlessness, you might feel closer

10. How might our personal study help us to imitate the faithful men and women in the Bible record?

11, 12. (a) How might you come to feel closer to Abram and Sarai? (b) How might you benefit from the example of Hannah, Elijah, or Samuel?

to Elijah as you study his plight and the way Jehovah comforted him. And youths who are bombarded by pressures from immoral schoolmates may feel closer to Samuel after studying how he handled the corrupt influence of Eli's sons at the tabernacle.

13 Does imitating the faith of such Bible characters somehow make you a mere imitation or less of an individual? Far from it! Remember, Jehovah's Word encourages us to imitate people of faith. (1 Cor. 4:16; 11:1; 2 Thess. 3:7, 9) What is more, some of the people whom we will study herein were themselves imitators of faithful ones who went before them. For instance, we note in Chapter 17 of this book that in her speech, Mary evidently drew on Hannah's words, clearly seeing her as an example. Did that make Mary's faith any less strong? Hardly! Rather, Hannah's example helped Mary to build faith so that she could make her own unique name with Jehovah God.

14 This book has been designed to help you strengthen your faith. The chapters that follow are a compilation of articles from the "Imitate Their Faith" series published in *The Watchtower* between 2008 and 2013.

However, some new material has been added. Questions are provided for discussion and application. Many colorful, detailed illustrations have been created for this volume, and existing ones have been enlarged and enhanced. Other helpful features, such as a time line and maps, have been included. *Imitate Their Faith* is a tool designed for personal, family, and congregation study. Many families might also enjoy simply reading the stories aloud together.

15 May this book help you to imitate the faith of Jehovah's loyal servants from the past. And may it help you to grow in faith as you draw closer to your heavenly Father, Jehovah!

---

13. Would imitating the faith of a Bible character somehow make you less of an individual? Explain.

14, 15. What are some features of this publication, and how can we make good use of it?

CONTENTS

CHAPTER ONE

"He, Although He Died, Yet Speaks"

ABEL looked at his flock of sheep grazing peacefully on the hillside. Then, perhaps he looked far beyond his sheep to a spot in the distance where he could just make out a faint glow. He knew that right there a flaming blade was turning, ever turning, blocking the way into the garden of Eden. His parents once lived there, but neither they nor their children could enter now. Imagine the late afternoon breeze ruffling Abel's hair as he turned his gaze upward and thought about his Creator. Would the breach between man and God ever be healed? Abel wanted nothing more than that.

² Abel speaks to you today. Can you hear him? You might say that such a thing is impossible. After all, this second son of Adam died a long time ago. His remains are long lost, mingled with the dust of nearly 60 centuries. Regarding the dead, the Bible teaches us: "They are conscious of nothing at all." (Eccl. 9:5, 10) Further, Abel never uttered a single word that is recorded in the Bible. So how can he speak to us?

³ The apostle Paul was inspired to say this about Abel: "Through it he, although he died, yet speaks." (**Read Hebrews 11:4.**) Through what does Abel speak? Through faith. Abel was the first human ever to develop that sterling quality. So powerfully did he demonstrate faith that his example is alive, a vibrant standard that we can apply today. If we learn from his faith and seek to imitate it, then the record of Abel is speaking to us in a very real and effective way.

⁴ What, though, can we learn of Abel and his faith when so little is said about him in the Bible? Let us see.

---

1. What prevented the family of Adam and Eve from entering the garden of Eden, and what did Abel want more than anything else?

2-4. In what sense does Abel speak to us today?

9

All his life, Abel could see that the cherubs were faithful and obedient servants of Jehovah

Growing Up in the Time of "the Founding of the World"

⁵ Abel was born near the dawn of human history. Jesus later associated Abel with "the founding of the world." (*Read Luke 11:50, 51.*) Jesus evidently meant the world of people who might be redeemed from sin. While Abel was the fourth human to exist, it seems that he was the first one whom God saw as redeemable.* Clearly, Abel did not grow up among the best of influences.

⁶ Though the world was young, a pall of sadness hung over the human family. Abel's parents, Adam and Eve, were likely beautiful, dynamic people. But they had fallen far in life, and they knew it. They were once perfect, with the prospect of eternal life before them. Then they rebelled against Jehovah God and were banished from their Paradise home in the garden of Eden. By putting their own desires ahead of all else—even the needs of their offspring—they lost perfection and eternal life.—Gen. 2:15–3:24.

⁷ Exiled to life outside the garden, Adam and Eve found their

---

* The expression "the founding of the world" involves the idea of casting down seed, suggesting procreation, so it has to do with the earliest human offspring. Why, though, did Jesus connect Abel with "the founding of the world" and not Cain, who was the first such offspring? Cain's decisions and actions amounted to a willful rebellion against Jehovah God. Like his parents, Cain does not appear to be in line for resurrection and redemption.

---

5. What is the meaning of Jesus' statement associating Abel with "the founding of the world"? (See also footnote.)

6. What kind of parents did Abel have?

7, 8. What did Eve say when Cain was born, and what may she have had in mind?

existence hard. Yet, when their first child was born, they named him Cain, or "Something Produced," and Eve proclaimed: "I have produced a man with the aid of Jehovah." Her words suggest that she may have had in mind the promise Jehovah made in the garden, foretelling that a certain woman would produce a "seed," or offspring, who would one day destroy the wicked one who had led Adam and Eve astray. (Gen. 3:15; 4:1) Did Eve imagine that she was the woman in the prophecy and that Cain was the promised "seed"?

8 If so, she was sadly mistaken. What is more, if she and Adam fed Cain such ideas as he grew up, they surely did his imperfect human pride no good. In time, Eve bore a second son, but we find no such high-flown statements about him. They named him Abel, which may mean "Exhalation," or "Vanity." (Gen. 4:2) Did that choice of a name reflect lower expectations, as if they put less hope in Abel than in Cain? We can only guess.

9 Parents today can learn much from those first parents. By your words and actions, will you feed your children's pride, ambition, and selfish tendencies? Or will you teach them to love Jehovah God and to seek friendship with him? Sadly, the first parents failed in their responsibility. Yet, there was hope for their offspring.

Abel Developed Faith—How?

10 As the two boys grew up, Adam likely trained them in work that was necessary to provide for the family. Cain took up farming; Abel took up shepherding.

11 However, Abel did something far more important. Over the years, he developed faith—that beautiful quality of which Paul later wrote. Think of it! Abel had no human example to whom he could look. How, then, did he develop faith in Jehovah God? Consider three solid bases on which his faith likely rested.

12 **Jehovah's creation.** True, Jehovah had placed a curse on the ground, causing it to produce thorns and thistles that impeded agriculture. Still, the earth generously produced the food that kept Abel's family alive. And there was no curse on the animals,

9. What can parents today learn from our first parents?

10, 11. Cain and Abel took up what kinds of work, and what quality did Abel develop?

12, 13. How might observing Jehovah's creation have helped Abel to grow in faith?

including birds and fish; nor on the mountains, lakes, rivers, and seas; nor on the skies, clouds, sun, moon, and stars. Everywhere Abel looked, he saw evidence of the profound love, wisdom, and goodness of Jehovah God, the one who created all things. (**Read Romans 1:20.**) No doubt, meditating appreciatively on such things strengthened Abel's faith.

invisible qualities

13 Abel surely took time to ponder spiritual matters. Picture him tending his flock. A shepherd's life required a great deal of walking. He led the gentle creatures over hills, through valleys, across rivers—ever seeking the greenest grass, the best watering holes, the most sheltered resting-places. Of all of God's creatures, sheep seemed the most helpless, as if they were designed to need man to guide and protect them. Did Abel see that he too needed guidance, protection, and care from Someone far wiser and more powerful than any human? No doubt he expressed many such thoughts in prayer, and his faith continued to grow as a result.

14 **Jehovah's promises.** Adam and Eve must have related to their sons the events in the garden of Eden that led to their expulsion. Thus, Abel had much food for meditation.

15 Jehovah said that the ground would be cursed. Abel could clearly see the thorns and thistles that fulfilled those words. Jehovah also foretold that Eve would suffer pain in pregnancy and childbirth. As Abel's siblings were born, he no doubt learned that those words came true as well. Jehovah foresaw that Eve would feel an unbalanced need for her husband's love and attention and that Adam would, in turn, dominate her. Abel watched that sad reality playing out before his eyes. In every case, Abel saw that Jehovah's word is completely reliable. Thus, Abel had solid reasons for putting faith in God's promise about a "seed," or offspring, who would one day right the wrongs that had begun in Eden.—Gen. 3:15-19.

14, 15. Jehovah's promises gave Abel what food for meditation?

16 Jehovah's servants. Abel did not find any good examples in the human family, but humans were not the only intelligent creatures on the earth at that time. When Adam and Eve were expelled from the garden, Jehovah made sure that neither they nor their offspring would gain access to that earthly Paradise. To guard the entrance, Jehovah posted cherubs—very high-ranking angels—along with the flaming blade of a sword that turned continually.—*Read Genesis 3:24.*

17 Imagine what it was like for Abel to see those cherubs when he was a boy. In their materialized form, their appearance surely bespoke immense power. And that "sword," ever aflame, ever turning, inspired awe as well. As Abel grew up, did he ever find that those cherubs got bored and left their post? No. Day and night, year after year, decade after decade, those intelligent, powerful creatures stayed right in that spot. Abel thus learned that Jehovah God had righteous, steadfast servants. In those cherubs, Abel could see a kind of loyalty and obedience to Jehovah that he could not find in his own family. That angelic example no doubt strengthened his faith.

18 Meditating on all that Jehovah revealed about himself through creation, divine promises, and the examples of His angelic servants, Abel found that his faith grew ever stronger. His

---

16, 17. What might Abel have learned from Jehovah's cherubs?

18. What ample basis do we have for building faith today?

In creation, Abel found a solid basis for faith in a loving Creator

example speaks to us, does it not? Young people in particular may find it reassuring to know that they can develop genuine faith in Jehovah God, no matter what their family members do. With the wonders of creation all around us and the entire Bible at our disposal, as well as many human examples of faith, we have ample basis for building faith today.

Abel's Sacrifice—Why It Excelled

19 As Abel's faith in Jehovah grew, he wanted to find a way to express that faith in action. Yet, what could a mere man give to the Creator of the universe? Clearly, God did not need any gift or help from humans. In time, Abel came to grasp a profound truth: If—with the right motive—he simply offered to Jehovah the best of what he had, his loving Father would be pleased.

20 Abel prepared to offer up some sheep from his flock. He selected the best, the firstlings, and what seemed the choicest pieces. Meanwhile, Cain too sought God's blessing and favor, preparing an offering from his crops. But his motives were not like those of Abel. The difference became apparent when the brothers presented their offerings.

21 Both sons of Adam may have used altars and fire for their offerings, perhaps within sight of the cherubs, who were the only living representatives of Jehovah on earth at that time. Jehovah responded! We read: "Jehovah was looking with favor upon Abel and his offering." (Gen. 4:4) How God made his favor evident, the Bible does not say.

22 Why did God favor Abel? Was it the offering itself? Abel did offer a living, breathing creature, shedding its precious life-blood. Did Abel realize how valuable such a sacrifice would be? Many centuries after Abel's time, God used the sacrifice of an un-blemished lamb to picture the sacrifice of His own perfect Son, "the Lamb of God," whose innocent blood would be shed. (John 1:29; Ex. 12:5-7) However, much of that surely lay well beyond Abel's knowledge or understanding.

23 What we know for certain is this: Abel offered up the very best of what he had. Jehovah looked with favor not only on the offering but on the man himself. Motivated by love for Jehovah and by genuine faith in him, Abel acted.

19. In time, what profound truth did Abel come to grasp?

20, 21. Cain and Abel each made what offering to Jehovah, and how did he respond?

22, 23. What accounts for the way Jehovah favored Abel's offering?

Abel offered his sacrifice in faith; Cain did not

grain offg.

24 It was different with Cain. Jehovah "did not look with any favor upon Cain and upon his offering." (Gen. 4:5) It was not that Cain's offering was faulty in itself; God's Law later allowed the offering of the produce of the ground. (Lev. 6:14, 15) But the Bible says of Cain that "his own works were wicked." (**Read 1 John 3:12.**) Like so many to this day, Cain evidently thought that the mere outward show of devotion to God was enough. His lack of real faith in or love for Jehovah quickly became apparent through his actions.

restored to favour

25 When Cain saw that he had not won Jehovah's favor, did he seek to learn from Abel's example? No. He seethed with hatred for his brother. Jehovah saw what was happening in Cain's heart and patiently tried to reason with him. He warned Cain that his course was leading toward serious sin, and He offered the hope of "an exaltation" if Cain would only change his ways. —Gen. 4:6, 7. *sin is crouching at the door*

26 Cain ignored God's warning. He invited his trusting younger brother to walk with him in the field. There Cain assaulted Abel and murdered him. (Gen. 4:8) In a sense, Abel thus became the first victim of religious persecution, the first martyr. He was dead, but his story was far from finished.

27 Figuratively, Abel's blood cried out to Jehovah God for vengeance, or justice. And God saw justice done, punishing wicked Cain for his crime. (Gen. 4:9-12) More important, the record of Abel's faith speaks to us today. His life span—perhaps about a century long—was short for humans of that era, but Abel made his years on this earth count. He died knowing that he had the love and approval of his heavenly Father, Jehovah. (Heb. 11:4) We can be confident, then, that he is safe in Jehovah's limitless memory, awaiting a resurrection to life in an earthly paradise. (John 5:28, 29) Will you meet him there? You can if you are determined to listen as Abel speaks and to imitate his outstanding faith.

TO THINK ABOUT . . .

- How does Abel speak to us today? *para 3.*
- What can parents learn from the mistakes of Abel's parents? *9*
- How might Jehovah's creation, his promises, and his cherubs have helped Abel to build faith? *12-17*
- In what ways do you intend to imitate Abel's faith? *23.*

24. (a) Why do we say that Cain's offering was not faulty in itself? (b) In what way was Cain like many to this day?

25, 26. Jehovah gave Cain what warning, yet what did Cain do?

27. (a) Why can we be confident that Abel is in line for a resurrection? (b) How can we be sure to meet Abel one day?

CHAPTER TWO

He "Walked With the True God"

NOAH straightened his back and stretched his aching muscles. Picture him seated on a broad wooden beam, taking a moment's rest from his work as he looked out over the immense structure of the ark. The pungent smell of hot tar was in the air; the sounds of woodworking tools reverberated. From where he sat, Noah could see his sons hard at work on various parts of the great network of timbers. His sons, their wives, and his own dear wife had all been laboring with him on this project for decades now. They had come a long way, but they had a long way to go!

² The people of the region thought of them all as fools. The more the ark took shape, the more the people laughed at the very thought of a deluge that would cover the whole earth. The disaster that Noah kept warning them about seemed so far-fetched, so preposterous! They could hardly believe that a man would waste his life—and the lives of his family—in such a foolish endeavor. However, Noah's God, Jehovah, saw the man in a very different light.

³ God's Word says: "Noah walked with the true God." (***Read Genesis 6:9.***) What did that mean? Not that God walked on earth, nor that Noah somehow went to heaven. Rather, Noah obeyed his God so closely and loved him so dearly that it was as if he and Jehovah walked together as friends. Thousands of years later, the Bible said of Noah: "Through [his] faith he condemned the world." (Heb. 11:7) How was that so? What can we today learn from his faith?

A Faultless Man in a Twisted World

⁴ Noah grew up in a world that was rapidly going from bad to worse. It had been bad in the days of his great-grandfather

---

1, 2. Noah and his family were involved in what project, and what were some of the challenges they faced?

3. In what sense did Noah walk with God?

4, 5. In Noah's day, how had the world gone from bad to worse?

17

Noah and his wife had to protect their children from bad influences

Enoch, another righteous man who walked with God. Enoch had foretold that a day of judgment was coming upon the ungodly people of the world. Now, in Noah's day, ungodliness was far worse. In fact, from Jehovah's viewpoint, the earth was ruined, for it was filled with violence. (Gen. 5:22; 6:11; Jude 14, 15) What had happened to make things so much worse?

⁵ A terrible tragedy had unfolded among God's spirit sons, the angels. One of them had already rebelled against Jehovah, becoming Satan the Devil by slandering God and luring Adam and Eve into sin. In Noah's day, other angels began to revolt against Jehovah's just rule. Forsaking their God-given station in heaven, they came to earth, assumed human form, and took beautiful women as their wives. Those proud, selfish rebel angels were a poisonous influence among humans.—Gen. 6:1, 2; Jude 6, 7.

⁶ Further, the unnatural unions between materialized angels and human women produced hybrid sons of extraordinary size and strength. The Bible calls them Nephilim, which literally means "Fellers"—those who cause others to fall. Vicious bullies, the Nephilim intensified the world's brutal, ungodly spirit. Little wonder that in the view of the Creator, "the badness of man was abundant in the earth and every inclination of the thoughts of his heart was only bad all the time." Jehovah determined that he would wipe out that wicked society in 120 years.—*Read Genesis 6:3-5.*

6. What effect did the Nephilim have on the world's spirit, and what did Jehovah determine to do?

18

7 Imagine trying to raise a family in such a world! Yet, Noah did so. He found a good wife. After Noah turned 500 years of age, his wife bore him three sons—Shem, Ham, and Japheth.* Together, the parents had to protect their boys from the vile influences surrounding them. Little boys tend to be filled with awe and admiration for "mighty ones" and "men of fame"—and the Nephilim were just that. Noah and his wife could hardly shield the children from every report about the exploits of those giants, but they could teach the appealing truth about Jehovah God, the one who hates all wickedness. They had to help their boys see that Jehovah felt hurt by the violence and rebellion in the world.—Gen. 6:6.

8 Parents today may well sympathize with Noah and his wife. Our world is likewise poisoned by violence and rebelliousness. Cities are often dominated by gangs of wayward youths. Even entertainment directed at young children may be saturated with violent themes. Wise parents do all they can to counter such influences by teaching their children about the God of peace, Jehovah, who will one day bring all violence to an end. (Ps. 11:5; 37:10, 11) Success is possible! Noah and his wife succeeded. Their boys grew up to be good men, and they married wives who were likewise willing to put the true God, Jehovah, first in their lives.

"Make for Yourself an Ark"

9 One day, Noah's life changed forever. Jehovah spoke to this beloved servant and told him of His purpose to bring the world of that time to an end. God commanded Noah: "Make for yourself an ark out of wood of a resinous tree."—Gen. 6:14.

10 This ark was not a ship, as some assume. It had neither bow nor stern, keel nor rudder—no curves. It was basically a great chest, or box. Jehovah gave Noah the precise dimensions of the ark, some details regarding its design, and directions to coat it inside and out with tar. And he told Noah why: "Here I am bringing the deluge of waters upon the earth . . . Everything that is in the earth will expire." However, Jehovah made this covenant, or formal agreement, with Noah: "You must go into the ark, you and your

---

* People in those early days lived far longer than we do today. Their longevity evidently had to do with their being closer to the vitality and perfection that Adam and Eve once had but lost.

7. Noah and his wife faced what challenge in protecting their sons from the vile influences of the day?

8. How can wise parents today imitate the example of Noah and his wife?

9, 10. (a) What command from Jehovah changed Noah's life? (b) What did Jehovah reveal to Noah about the ark's design and purpose?

sons and your wife and your sons' wives with you." Noah was also to bring representatives of all kinds of animals. Only those aboard the ark could survive the coming Deluge!—Gen. 6:17-20.

¹¹ Noah faced a gigantic task. This ark was to be enormous —some 437 feet long, 73 feet wide, and 44 feet tall. It was far larger than the largest seagoing wooden ships built even in modern times. Did Noah back off from this assignment, complain about its challenges, or alter the details to make it easier on himself? The Bible answers: "Noah proceeded to do according to all that God had commanded him. He did just so."—Gen. 6:22.

¹² The work took decades, perhaps 40 to 50 years. There were trees to fell, logs to haul, and beams to hew, shape, and join. The ark was to have three stories, or decks, a number of compartments, and a door in the side. Evidently, there were windows along the top, as well as a roof that likely peaked in the middle with a slight pitch so that water would run off.—Gen. 6:14-16.

¹³ As the years passed and the ark took shape, Noah must have been so glad to have the support of his family! There was another aspect to the work that might have been even more challenging than ark-building. The Bible tells us that Noah was "a preacher of righteousness." (**Read 2 Peter 2:5.**) So he courageously took the lead in trying to warn the people of that wicked, godless society about the destruction that was heading their way. How did they respond? Jesus Christ later recalled that time, saying that those people "took no note." He said that they were so caught up in the affairs of daily life—eating, drinking, and marrying—that they paid no heed to Noah. (Matt. 24:37-39) No doubt many ridiculed him and his family; some may have threatened him and violently opposed him. They may even have tried to sabotage the construction project.

¹⁴ Yet, Noah and his family never quit. Even though they lived in a world that was geared toward making their primary pursuit in life seem trivial, misguided, or foolish, they still kept at it faithfully. Christian families today can thus learn a great deal from the faith of Noah and his family. After all, we live in what the Bible calls "the last days" of this world system of things. (2 Tim. 3:1) Jesus said that our era would be just like the era in which Noah built

11, 12. Noah faced what gigantic task, and how did he respond to the challenge?

13. What aspect of Noah's work may have been more challenging than ark-building, and how did people respond to it?

14. What can Christian families today learn from Noah and his family?

Noah and his family worked together to fulfill God's commands

Despite evidence of God's blessing on Noah, people ridiculed him and ignored his message

the ark. If the world reacts to the message about God's Kingdom with apathy, ridicule, or even persecution, Christians do well to remember Noah. They are not the first to face such challenges.

"Go . . . Into the Ark"

¹⁵ Decades passed, and the ark gradually assumed its final shape. As Noah neared his 600th year, he dealt with losses. His father, Lamech, died.* Five years later, Lamech's father, Noah's grandfather Methuselah, died at the age of 969—ending the longest human life in the Bible record. (Gen. 5:27) Both Methuselah and Lamech had been contemporaries of the first man, Adam.

¹⁶ In his 600th year, the patriarch Noah received a new message from Jehovah God: "Go, you and all your household, into the ark." At the same time, God told Noah to take all the kinds of animals into the ark—by sevens in the case of the clean ones, fit for sacrificial use, and the rest by twos.—Gen. 7:1-3.

¹⁷ It must have been an unforgettable sight. From the horizon they streamed in by the thousands—walking, flying, crawling, wad-

---

* Lamech had given his son the name Noah—probably meaning "Rest" or "Consolation"—and had prophesied that Noah would fulfill the significance of his name by leading mankind to a rest from toiling on cursed ground. (Gen. 5:28, 29) Lamech did not live to see his prophecy fulfilled. Noah's mother, brothers, and sisters may have perished in the Flood.

15. Noah dealt with what losses as he neared his 600th year?

16, 17. (a) Noah received what new message in his 600th year? (b) Describe the unforgettable sight that Noah and his family witnessed.

dling, lumbering—all in an astonishing variety of sizes, shapes, and dispositions. We need not imagine poor Noah trying to corral, wrangle, or somehow cajole all those wild animals into entering the confined space of the ark. The account says that "they *went in* . . . to Noah inside the ark."—Gen. 7:9.

[18] Some skeptics might ask: 'How could such a thing happen? And how could all those animals coexist peacefully in a confined space?' Consider: Is it really beyond the power of the Creator of the entire universe to control his animal creations, even render them tame and docile if needed? Remember, Jehovah is the God who created the animals. Much later, he also parted the Red Sea and made the sun stand still. Could he not carry out every event described in Noah's account? Of course he could, and he did!

[19] Granted, God could have chosen to save his animal creations in some other way. However, he wisely chose a way that reminds us of the trust that he originally placed in humans to take care of all the living things on this earth. (Gen. 1:28) Many parents today thus use Noah's story to teach their children that Jehovah values the animals and the people he has created.

[20] Jehovah told Noah that the Deluge would come in a week.

18, 19. (a) How might we reason on the questions that skeptics raise regarding the events in Noah's account? (b) How do we see Jehovah's wisdom in the way that he chose to save his animal creations?

20. How might Noah and his family have been occupied during the final week before the Deluge?

It must have been a hectic time for the family. Imagine the work of getting all the animals as well as foodstuffs for the animals and for the family placed in an orderly fashion and hauling the family's belongings aboard. Noah's wife and the wives of Shem, Ham, and Japheth may have been especially concerned about making a livable home in that ark.

21 What of the community? They still "took no note"—even in the face of all the evidence that Jehovah was blessing Noah and his endeavors. They could not help but notice the animals streaming into the ark. But we should not be surprised at their apathy. People today likewise take no note of the overwhelming evidence that we are now living in the final days of this world system of things. And as the apostle Peter foretold, ridiculers have come with their ridicule, mocking those who heed God's warning. (*Read 2 Peter 3: 3-6.*) Likewise, people surely ridiculed Noah and his family.

22 When did the ridicule end? The account tells us that once Noah had brought his family and the animals inside the ark, "Jehovah shut the door behind him." If any ridiculers were nearby, that divine action no doubt silenced them. If not, the rain did—for down it came! And it kept coming, and coming, and coming—flooding the whole world, just as Jehovah had said.—Gen. 7:16-21.

23 Did Jehovah take delight in the death of those wicked people? No! (Ezek. 33:11) On the contrary, he had given them ample opportunity to change their ways and do what was right. Could they have done so? Noah's life course answered that question. By walking with Jehovah, obeying his God in all things, Noah showed that survival was possible. In that sense, his faith condemned the world of his day; it cast the wickedness of his generation in a clear light. His faith kept him and his family safe. If you imitate the faith of Noah, you may likewise do yourself and those you love a world of good. Like Noah, you can walk with Jehovah God as your Friend. And the friendship can last forever!

TO THINK ABOUT . . .

- Noah and his wife faced what challenges in raising their children?

- How did Noah show faith in building the ark?

- Why must preaching have been a difficult assignment in Noah's day?

- In what ways are you determined to imitate the faith of Noah?

21, 22. (a) Why should we not be surprised at the apathy of the community in Noah's day? (b) When did the ridicule that Noah and his family received from their neighbors come to an end?

23. (a) How do we know that Jehovah took no delight in the death of the wicked in Noah's day? (b) Why is it wise to imitate the faith of Noah today?

CHAPTER THREE

"The Father of All Those Having Faith"

ABRAM looked up, his gaze drawn to the ziggurat that loomed over his home city of Ur.* There was a clamor up there, and smoke was rising. The priests of the moon god were offering sacrifices again. Picture Abram turning away and shaking his head, a frown creasing his brow. As he made his way homeward through the throngs on the streets, he likely thought about the idolatry that pervaded Ur. How the stain of that corrupt worship had spread in the world since Noah's day!

How did Abram become such an outstanding example of faith?

² Noah died just two years before Abram was born. When Noah and his family emerged from the ark after the great Deluge, that patriarch offered up a sacrifice to Jehovah God, who, in turn, made a rainbow appear. (Gen. 8:20; 9:12-14) At that time, the only worship in the world was pure worship. But now, as the tenth generation from Noah was spreading abroad in the earth, pure worship was becoming a rarity. People everywhere were worshipping pagan gods. Even Abram's father, Terah, was involved in idolatry, perhaps making idols.—Josh. 24:2.

³ Abram was different. As his life went on, he stood out more and more because of his faith. In fact, the apostle Paul was later inspired to call him "the father of all those having faith"! (**Read Romans 4:11.**) Let us see how Abram began his journey

---

* Years later, God changed Abram's name to Abraham, meaning "Father of a Multitude."—Gen. 17:5.

1, 2. How had the world changed since Noah's day, and how was Abram affected?

3. As Abram's life went on, what quality stood out in him, and what can we learn from that?

Abram rejected the idolatry so prevalent in Ur

to become such a man. We ourselves can thereby learn much about how to grow in faith.

Serving Jehovah in the Post-Flood World

⁴ How did Abram come to learn about Jehovah God? We know that Jehovah had faithful servants on earth in those days. Shem was such a man. Though not the eldest of Noah's three sons, he is often mentioned first. That was evidently because Shem was a man of outstanding faith.* Some time after the Flood, Noah referred to Jehovah as "Shem's God." (Gen. 9:26) Shem showed respect for Jehovah and for pure worship.

⁵ Did Abram know Shem? It is possible that he did. Imagine Abram as a boy. How fascinated he would have been to learn that he had a living ancestor whose ancient, wise eyes had witnessed over four centuries of human history! Shem had seen the evils of the pre-Flood world, the great Deluge that cleansed the earth, the founding of the first nations as mankind multiplied in the earth, and the dark days of Nimrod's rebellion at the Tower of Babel. Faithful Shem stayed clear of that rebellion, so when Jehovah confused the language of the tower-builders, Shem and his family continued to speak man's original language, the tongue of Noah. That family included Abram. Surely, then, Abram grew up with a high regard for Shem. What is more, Shem remained alive through most of Abram's long life. So Abram may have learned about Jehovah from Shem.

⁶ In any event, Abram took to heart the great lesson of the Deluge. He endeavored to walk with God as Noah had walked with Him. That is why Abram rejected idolatry and stood out as different in Ur, perhaps even in his immediate family. However, he came to find a wonderful ally in life. He married Sarai, a woman who was exceptional not only for her beauty but also for her

---

* Similarly, Abram is often mentioned first among Terah's sons, although he was far from being the eldest.

4, 5. From whom might Abram have learned about Jehovah, and why may we conclude that this is a possibility?

6. (a) How did Abram show that he had taken to heart the great lesson of the Deluge? (b) What kind of life did Abram and Sarai have together?

great faith in Jehovah.* Though childless, that couple no doubt found much joy in serving Jehovah together. They also adopted Abram's orphaned nephew, Lot.

7 Abram never left Jehovah for the idolatry of Ur. He and Sarai were willing to stand out as different from that idolatrous community. If we are to develop genuine faith, we need a similar spirit. We too must be willing to be different. Jesus said that his followers would be "no part of the world" and that the world would hate them as a result. (*Read John 15:19.*) If you ever feel the pain of rejection by members of your family or your community because of your decision to serve Jehovah, remember that you are not alone. You are in good company, walking with God as did Abram and Sarai before you.

"Go Out From Your Land"

8 One day, Abram had an unforgettable experience. He received a communication from Jehovah God! The Bible provides little in the way of specifics, but it does say that "the God of glory" appeared to that faithful man. (*Read Acts 7:2, 3.*) Perhaps by means of an angelic representative, Abram received a glimpse of the overwhelming glory of the Sovereign of the universe. We can only imagine how thrilled Abram was to see the contrast between the living God and the lifeless idols worshipped among his contemporaries.

9 What was Jehovah's message to Abram? "Go out from your land and from your relatives and come on into the land I shall show you." Jehovah did not say *which* land he had in mind —only that he would show it to Abram. First, though, Abram would have to leave behind his homeland and his relatives. In the cultures of the ancient Middle East, family meant a great deal. For a man to leave his relatives and move far away was often considered a terrible fate; to some, worse than death itself!

10 Leaving his land involved sacrifice. Ur was evidently a bustling, wealthy city. (See the box "The City That Abram and Sarai Left Behind.") Excavations have revealed that very comfortable

---

* Later, God changed Sarai's name to Sarah, meaning "Princess."—Gen. 17:15.

---

7. How do followers of Jesus need to imitate Abram?

8, 9. (a) Abram had what unforgettable experience? (b) What was Jehovah's message to Abram?

10. Why might it have been a sacrifice for Abram and Sarai to leave their home in Ur?

homes existed in ancient Ur; some had a dozen or more rooms for family and servants, all arranged around a paved inner courtyard. Common amenities included water fountains, lavatories, and waste disposal. Remember, too, that Abram and Sarai were far from young; he was likely in his 70's, she in her 60's. He surely wanted Sarai to be reasonably comfortable and well cared for—what any good husband wants for his wife. Imagine their conversations about this assignment, the questions and concerns that might have arisen in their hearts. Abram must have been so pleased when Sarai rose to this challenge! Like him, she was willing to leave all the comforts of home behind.

¹¹ With the decision made, Abram and Sarai had much to do. A great deal of packing and organizing lay ahead of them. What would they take on this journey into the unknown, and what would they leave behind? More important, though, were the people in their lives. What would they do about aged Terah? They decided to take him and care for him along the way. He may have consented heartily, for the account credits him, as patriarch, with taking his family out of Ur. No doubt he had given up idolatry. Abram's nephew Lot would also accompany the sojourners. —Gen. 11:31.

¹² Finally, the morning of departure was upon them. Picture the caravan assembling outside the city walls and moat of Ur. The camels and donkeys were laden, the flocks were assembled, the family and servants were settled into their places, and a sense of expectation was in the air.* Perhaps all eyes turned to Abram, waiting for him to give the signal to go. Finally, the moment arrived, and they set off, leaving Ur behind forever.

¹³ Today, many servants of Jehovah decide to move to where there is a need for more Kingdom preachers. Others decide to learn a new language in order to expand their ministry. Or they decide to try some form of service that is outside their comfort zone. Such decisions generally require sacrifice—a willingness to forgo some measure of material comfort. How commendable that spirit is, and how like the spirit of Abram and Sarai! If we

* Some scholars question whether the camel was domesticated in Abram's time. However, the grounds for such objections are weak. The Bible several times mentions camels among Abram's possessions.—Gen. 12:16; 24:35.

11, 12. (a) What preparations and decisions needed to be made prior to leaving Ur? (b) How might we picture the morning of departure?
13. How do many servants of Jehovah today show a spirit similar to that of Abram and Sarai?

show such faith, we may be assured that Jehovah will always give us far more than we give him. He never fails to reward faith. (Heb. 6:10; 11:6) Did he do so for Abram?

Crossing the Euphrates

14 The caravan gradually settled into the routine of travel. We might imagine Abram and Sarai alternating between riding and walking, their conversation mingling with the tinkling of bells hanging from the animals' harnesses. Gradually, even the less experienced travelers became more adept at making and breaking camp and helping aged Terah to get comfortably situated atop a camel or a donkey. They made their way northwest, following the great arc of the Euphrates River. Days stretched into weeks, and the landscape slid slowly by.

15 Finally, after some 600 miles on the road, they reached the beehive-shaped huts of Haran, a prosperous city on a crossroads of the East-West trade routes. There the family stopped, and there they settled for a time. Perhaps Terah was too frail to travel any farther.

14, 15. What was the journey from Ur to Haran like, and why might Abram have decided to settle in Haran for a time?

The City That Abram and Sarai Left Behind

Jehovah's organization has long worked hard to bring color and life to discussions of Bible characters and their background. For example, this description of the city that Abram and Sarai left behind appeared in the May 22, 1988, issue of *Awake!* magazine:

"HALFWAY between the Persian Gulf and the city of Baghdad there is an unsightly pile of mud bricks. It is but a lonely sentinel keeping watch over a vast stretch of sterile desert. Pummeled by dust storms and baked by a hostile sun, the brooding ruins sit in austere silence that is broken only by the occasional howl of a nocturnal creature. This is all that remains of the once mighty city of Ur.

"But go back four millenniums. There, on what was then the eastern bank of the Euphrates River, Ur is a thriving city! Gleaming whitewashed houses and shops line its winding streets. Merchants and patrons haggle over prices in the bazaars. Workers labor day and night spinning milk-white thread from billowy bundles of wool. Slaves tramp down creaking ships' ramps, bowing under the weight of imported treasures.

"All this bustle takes place in the shadow of a towering ziggurat that dominates the city's landscape. Worshippers come to this sanctuary to render homage to a deity they believe has brought prosperity to Ur—the moon-god Nanna, or Sin.

"To one man, though, the odor of sacrifices offered atop this massive pyramid is an unholy stench. His name is Abram."

16 In time, Terah died at the age of 205. (Gen. 11:32) Abram found great comfort during that time of loss, for Jehovah again communicated with him. He repeated the instructions that he had given back in Ur, and he enlarged on his promises. Abram was to become "a great nation," and blessings would become available to all the families on earth because of him. (*Read Genesis 12:2, 3.*) Thrilled over this covenant between him and God, Abram knew that it was time to move on.

17 This time, though, there was even more to pack, for Jehovah had blessed Abram during his stay in Haran. The account mentions "all the goods that they had accumulated and the souls whom they had acquired in Haran." (Gen. 12:5) To become a nation, Abram would need material resources and servants—a large household. Jehovah does not always make his servants rich, but he does give them whatever they need in order to accomplish his will. Thus fortified, Abram led his caravan into the unknown.

18 Several days' journey from Haran lay Carchemish, where caravans commonly crossed the Euphrates. Perhaps it was at this spot that Abram reached a milestone in the history of God's dealings with His people. It was evidently on the 14th day of the month later named Nisan, in 1943 B.C.E., that Abram led his caravan across the river. (Ex. 12:40-43) To the south stretched the land that Jehovah had promised to show Abram. On that day, God's covenant with Abram went into effect.

19 Abram moved southward through the land, and the caravan stopped near the big trees of Moreh, near Shechem.

A Vital Date in Bible History

The date on which Abram crossed the Euphrates River is important in Bible chronology. Other key events transpired on that date in later years. Exactly 430 years later, on Nisan 14, 1513 B.C.E., Jehovah freed Israel from bondage to Egypt so that they could go and claim the land that God had promised to Abram. (Ex. 12:40, 41; Gal. 3:17) And on that same date in 33 C.E., Jesus gathered his apostles together and established with them a covenant that made them part of a government in heaven that will soon solve all mankind's ills. (Luke 22:29) To this day, Jehovah's Witnesses gather each year to commemorate the Lord's Evening Meal on the same date of the Jewish calendar—Nisan 14. —Luke 22:19.

16, 17. (a) Abram was thrilled by what covenant? (b) How did Jehovah bless Abram during his stay in Haran?

18. (a) When did Abram reach a milestone in the history of God's dealings with His people? (b) What other important events transpired on Nisan 14 in later years? (See the box "A Vital Date in Bible History.")

19. Jehovah's promise to Abram included a mention of what, and of what might that have reminded Abram?

Leaving behind their comfortable life in Ur presented challenges to Abram and Sarai

There Abram once more received word from Jehovah. God's promise this time mentioned Abram's seed, or progeny, who would take possession of the land. Did Abram think back to the prophecy Jehovah had uttered in Eden, the one mentioning a "seed," or offspring, who would one day rescue mankind? (Gen. 3:15; 12:7) Perhaps. He may have begun to see, however dimly, that he was part of a grand purpose that Jehovah had in mind.

[20] Abram deeply appreciated the privilege that Jehovah bestowed on him. As he moved through the land—no doubt cautiously, since it was still inhabited by the Canaanites—Abram stopped and built altars to Jehovah, first near the big trees of Moreh, then near Bethel. He called on the name of Jehovah, likely expressing his heartfelt thanks to his God as he contemplated the future of his progeny. He may also have preached to his Canaanite neighbors. (*Read Genesis 12:7, 8.*) Of course, great challenges to Abram's faith lay ahead on his life's journey. Wisely, Abram was not looking back to the home and comforts he had left behind in Ur. He was looking forward. Hebrews 11:10 says of Abram: "He was awaiting the city having real foundations, the builder and maker of which city is God."

[21] We who serve Jehovah today know a lot more about that figurative city—God's Kingdom—than did Abram. We know that the Kingdom is reigning in heaven and will soon bring an end to this world system, and we know that Abram's long-promised Seed, Jesus Christ, now rules that Kingdom. What a privilege it will be for us to see the time when Abraham lives again and at last grasps the divine purpose that he could formerly see only in hazy outline! Would you like to see Jehovah fulfill his every promise? By all means, then, continue to do what Abram did. Show a spirit of self-sacrifice, obedience, and prayerful appreciation for the privileges Jehovah extends to you. As you imitate Abram's faith, "the father of all those having faith" will, in a sense, become your father too!

TO THINK ABOUT . . .

- How did Abram show faith when it came to idolatry?

- What impresses you about Abram's willingness to leave Ur?

- Abram's faith brought him what blessings and privileges?

- In what ways would you like to imitate the faith of Abram?

---

20. How did Abram show appreciation for the privilege that Jehovah bestowed on him?

21. How does our knowledge of God's Kingdom compare with that of Abram, and what are you motivated to do?

CHAPTER FOUR

"Where You Go I Shall Go"

RUTH walked beside Naomi on a road that stretched across the high, windswept plains of Moab. They were alone now, two tiny figures in a vast landscape. Imagine Ruth noticing that the afternoon shadows had lengthened, then looking at her mother-in-law and wondering if it was time to find a place to rest for the night. She loved Naomi dearly and would do all she could to care for her.

2 Each woman bore a heavy burden of grief. Naomi had been a widow for years now, but she was mourning more recent losses—the deaths of her two sons, Chilion and Mahlon. Ruth too was grieving. Mahlon was her husband. She and Naomi were heading to the same destination, the town of Bethlehem in Israel. In a way, though, their journeys differed. Naomi was going home. Ruth was venturing into the unknown, leaving her own kin, her homeland, and all its customs—including its gods—behind her.—*Read Ruth 1:3-6.*

3 What would move a young woman to make such a drastic change? How would Ruth find the strength to make a new life for herself and to take care of Naomi? In learning the answers, we will find much to imitate in the faith of Ruth the Moabitess. (See also the box "A Masterpiece in Miniature.") First, let us consider how those two women came to be on that long road to Bethlehem.

A Family Torn Apart by Tragedy

4 Ruth grew up in Moab, a small country that lay to the east of the Dead Sea. The region consisted mostly of high, sparsely

---

1, 2. (a) Describe the journey of Ruth and Naomi and the burden of grief they carried. (b) How did Ruth's journey differ from that of Naomi?

3. The answers to what questions will help us to imitate the faith of Ruth?

4, 5. (a) Why did Naomi's family move to Moab? (b) What challenges did Naomi face in Moab?

Ruth wisely drew close to Naomi during a time of grief and loss

wooded tablelands cut through by deep ravines. "The fields of Moab" often proved to be fertile farmland, even when famine stalked Israel. That, in fact, was why Ruth first came into contact with Mahlon and his family.—Ruth 1:1.

5 A famine in Israel had convinced Naomi's husband, Elimelech, that he must move his wife and two sons away from their homeland and take up living in Moab as aliens. The move must have presented challenges to the faith of each family member, for Israelites needed to worship regularly at the sacred place Jehovah had designated. (Deut. 16:16, 17) Naomi managed to keep her faith alive. Still, she was grief-stricken when her husband died.—Ruth 1:2, 3.

6 Naomi might well have suffered again later when her sons married Moabite women. (Ruth 1:4) She knew that her nation's forefather, Abraham, went to great lengths to procure a wife for his son, Isaac, from among his own people, who worshipped Jehovah. (Gen. 24:3, 4) Later, the Mosaic Law warned the Israelites not to let their sons and daughters marry foreigners, for fear that God's people would be led into idolatry.—Deut. 7:3, 4.

7 Nevertheless, Mahlon and Chilion married Moabite women. If Naomi was concerned or disappointed, she evidently made sure that she showed her daughters-in-law, Ruth and Orpah, genuine kindness and love. Perhaps she hoped that they too would someday come to worship Jehovah as she did. At any rate, both Ruth and Orpah were fond of Naomi. That good relationship helped them when tragedy struck. Before either of the young women had borne children, both became widows.—Ruth 1:5.

8 Did Ruth's religious background prepare her for such a tragedy? It is hard to see how it could have. The Moabites worshipped many gods, the chief among them being Chemosh. (Num. 21:29) It seems that the Moabite religion was not exempt from the brutality and horrors common in those times, including the sacrifice of children. Anything Ruth learned from Mahlon or Naomi about the loving and merciful God of Israel, Jehovah, surely struck her as a marked contrast. Jehovah ruled through love, not terror. (*Read Deuteronomy 6:5.*) In the wake of her devastating loss, Ruth may have drawn even closer to Naomi and listened willingly to the older woman as she spoke

---

6, 7. (a) Why might Naomi have been concerned when her sons married Moabite women? (b) Why was Naomi's treatment of her daughters-in-law commendable?

8. What may have drawn Ruth to Jehovah?

about the almighty God, Jehovah, his wonderful works, and the loving, merciful way he dealt with his people.

9 Naomi, for her part, was eager for news of her homeland. One day she heard, perhaps from a traveling merchant, that the famine in Israel was over. Jehovah had turned his attention to his people. Bethlehem was again living up to its name, which means "House of Bread." Naomi decided to return home.—Ruth 1:6.

10 What would Ruth and Orpah do? (Ruth 1:7) They had grown close to Naomi through their shared ordeal. Ruth in particular, it seems, was drawn to Naomi's kindness and her steadfast faith in Jehovah. The three widows set off for Judah together.

11 The account of Ruth reminds us that tragedy and loss beset good, honest people as well as bad. (Eccl. 9:2, 11) It shows us too that in the face of unbearable loss, we are wise to seek comfort and solace in others—especially those who seek refuge in Jehovah, the God whom Naomi worshipped.—Prov. 17:17.

The Loyal Love of Ruth

12 As the miles stretched out behind the three widows, another concern began weighing on Naomi. She thought of the two young women at her side and of the love they had shown to her and her sons. She could not bear the thought of adding to their burdens now. If they left their homeland and came with her, what could she do for them in Bethlehem?

13 Finally, Naomi spoke up: "Go, return each one to the house of her mother. May Jehovah exercise loving-kindness toward you, just as you have exercised it toward the men now dead and toward me." She also expressed a hope that Jehovah would reward them with new husbands and new lives. "Then she kissed

---

9-11. (a) What decision did Naomi, Ruth, and Orpah make? (b) What can we learn from the tragedies that befell Naomi, Ruth, and Orpah?

12, 13. Why did Naomi want Ruth and Orpah to go back to their homes instead of accompanying her, and how did the two young women react at first?

them," the account says, "and they began to raise their voices and weep." It is not hard to see why Ruth and Orpah felt so attached to this kindhearted and unselfish woman. Both of them kept insisting: "No, but with you we shall return to your people."—Ruth 1:8-10.

14 Naomi was not so easily persuaded, though. She reasoned forcefully that there was little that she could do for them in Israel, since she had no husband to provide for her, no sons for them to marry, and no prospects of either. She revealed that her inability to care for them was a source of real bitterness to her. With Orpah, Naomi's words hit home. She had family there in Moab, a mother, and a home that was waiting for her. It really did seem more practical to remain in Moab. So, with a heavy heart, she kissed Naomi good-bye and turned away.—Ruth 1: 11-14.

15 What about Ruth? Naomi's arguments applied to her as well. Yet, we read: "As for Ruth, she stuck with her." Perhaps Naomi had resumed walking on the road when she noticed that Ruth was trailing behind her. She remonstrated: "Look! Your widowed sister-in-law has returned to her people and her gods. Return with your widowed sister-in-law." (Ruth 1:15) Naomi's words reveal a vital detail to the reader. Orpah had returned not only to her people but also to "her gods." She was content to remain a worshipper of Chemosh and other false gods. Was that how Ruth felt?

14, 15. (a) To what did Orpah return? (b) How did Naomi try to persuade Ruth to leave her?

"Your people will be my people, and your God my God"

16 As she faced Naomi on that lonely road, Ruth's heart was sure and clear. It swelled with love for Naomi—and for the God whom Naomi served. So Ruth spoke: "Do not plead with me to abandon you, to turn back from accompanying you; for where you go I shall go, and where you spend the night I shall spend the night. Your people will be my people, and your God my God. Where you die I shall die, and there is where I shall be buried. May Jehovah do so to me and add to it if anything but death should make a separation between me and you."—Ruth 1:16, 17.

17 Ruth's words are remarkable—so much so that they have long outlived her, echoing down through some 30 centuries. They perfectly reveal a precious quality, loyal love. The love that Ruth felt was so strong and so loyal that she would stick with Naomi wherever she went. Only death could separate them. Naomi's people would become her own people, for Ruth was ready to leave behind everything she knew in Moab—even the Moabite gods. Unlike Orpah, Ruth could wholeheartedly say that she wanted Naomi's God, Jehovah, to be her own God as well.*

18 So they traveled on, just the two of them now, on the long road to Bethlehem. By one estimate, the journey might have taken as long as a week. Surely, though, each found in the company of the other some measure of comfort in the face of grief.

19 There is no shortage of grief in this world. In our own times, which the Bible calls "critical times hard to deal with," we face all manner of losses as well as grief. (2 Tim. 3:1) The quality we find in Ruth has thus become more important than ever. Loyal love—the kind of love that holds on to its object and simply refuses to let go—is a powerful force for good in this darkening world. We need it in marriage, we need it in family relations, we need it in friendships, we need it in the Christian congregation. (*Read 1 John 4:7, 8, 20.*) As we cultivate that kind of love, we are imitating the outstanding example of Ruth.

---

* It is noteworthy that Ruth did not use only the impersonal title "God," as many foreigners might; she also used God's personal name, Jehovah. *The Interpreter's Bible* comments: "The writer thus emphasizes that this foreigner is a follower of the true God."

16-18. (a) How did Ruth demonstrate loyal love? (b) What can we learn from Ruth about loyal love? (See also the pictures of the two women.)

19. How do you think we can imitate Ruth's loyal love in our family, among our friends, and in the congregation?

Ruth and Naomi in Bethlehem

20 It is, of course, one thing to put loyal love into words; it is quite another to prove the quality in action. Ruth had before her the opportunity to show her loyal love not only to Naomi but also to the God whom she chose as her own, Jehovah.

21 The two women finally reached Bethlehem, a village about six miles south of Jerusalem. Naomi and her family, it seems, had once been quite prominent in that little town, for the whole place was buzzing with the news of Naomi's return. The women there would peer at her and say, "Is this Naomi?" Evidently, her sojourn in Moab had left her much changed; her countenance and bearing showed the mark of years of hardship and grief. —Ruth 1:19.

22 To those kinswomen and neighbors of years past, Naomi revealed how bitter her life had become to her. She even felt that her name should be changed from Naomi, which means "My Pleasantness," to Mara, which means "Bitter." Poor Naomi! Much like Job before her, she believed that Jehovah God had brought her hardships on her. —Ruth 1:20, 21; Job 2:10; 13:24-26.

23 As the two women settled into life in Bethlehem, Ruth began thinking about how best to take care of herself and Naomi. She learned that the Law that Jehovah had given to his people in Israel included a loving provision for the poor. They were allowed to go into the fields at harvesttime and follow the reapers, gleaning what was left behind as well as what grew at the edges and corners of the fields.*—Lev. 19:9, 10; Deut. 24:19-21.

---

* It was a remarkable law, surely unlike anything Ruth knew in her homeland. In the ancient Near East in those days, widows were treated badly. Notes one reference work: "After her husband's death, normally a widow had to rely on her sons for support; if she had none, she might have to sell herself into slavery, resort to prostitution, or die."

20-22. (a) How had Naomi's life in Moab affected her? (b) Naomi held what mistaken view of her hardships? (See also James 1:13.)

23. What did Ruth begin to think about, and what provision did the Mosaic Law make for the poor? (See also footnote.)

A Masterpiece in Miniature

The book of Ruth has been described as a small gem, a masterpiece in miniature. Granted, the book has neither the sweep nor the scope of the book of Judges, which precedes it and provides the time setting for Ruth. (Ruth 1:1) Both books were evidently written by the prophet Samuel. Yet, as you read through the Bible, you may agree that the book of Ruth is beautifully placed in the Bible canon. After reading of the wars, raids, and counterraids recorded in the book of Judges, you come to this little book that reminds us that Jehovah never loses sight of peaceable people struggling with everyday problems. This simple domestic drama offers profound lessons about love, loss, faith, and loyalty that can benefit us all.

²⁴ It was the time of the barley harvest, likely in April by our modern calendar, and Ruth went to the fields to see who would let her work under the provision for gleaners. She chanced upon the fields of a man named Boaz, a wealthy landowner and a relative of Naomi's dead husband, Elimelech. Though the Law gave her the right to glean, she did not take it for granted; she asked the young man in charge of the harvesters for permission to work. He granted it, and then Ruth got right to work.—Ruth 1:22–2:3, 7.

²⁵ Imagine Ruth following the harvesters. As they cut through the barley with their flint sickles, she stooped to pick up what they dropped or left behind, bundled the stalks into sheaves, and carried them off to a spot where she could beat out the grain later. It was slow, tiring work, and it got harder as the morning wore on. Yet, Ruth kept at it, stopping only to wipe the sweat from her brow and to eat a simple lunch in "the house" —likely a shelter set up to provide shade for the workers.

²⁶ Ruth probably neither hoped nor expected to be noticed, but she was. Boaz saw her and asked the young foreman who she was. A remarkable man of faith, Boaz greeted his workers—some of whom may have been day laborers or even foreigners—with the words: "Jehovah be with you." And they responded in kind. This spiritually-minded older man took a fatherly interest in Ruth.—Ruth 2:4-7.

24, 25. What did Ruth do when she chanced upon the fields of Boaz, and what was the gleaning work like?

26, 27. What kind of a person was Boaz, and how did he treat Ruth?

Ruth was willing to do hard, humble work to provide for herself and Naomi

²⁷ Calling her "my daughter," Boaz advised Ruth to keep coming to his fields to glean and to stay near the young women of his household to avoid being harassed by any of the workmen. He made sure that she had food to eat at lunchtime. (**Read Ruth 2:8, 9, 14.**) Above all, though, he sought to commend and encourage her. How so?

²⁸ When Ruth asked Boaz what she, a foreigner, had done to deserve his kind favor, he replied that he had heard about all that she had done for her mother-in-law, Naomi. Likely Naomi had praised her beloved Ruth among the women of Bethlehem, and word had reached Boaz. He knew, too, that Ruth had turned to the worship of Jehovah, for he said: "May Jehovah reward the way you act, and may there come to be a perfect wage for you from Jehovah the God of Israel, under whose wings you have come to seek refuge."—Ruth 2:12.

²⁹ How those words must have encouraged Ruth! She had, indeed, decided to take refuge under the wings of Jehovah God, like a young bird securely nestled against a protective parent. She thanked Boaz for speaking to her so reassuringly. And she kept on working until evening fell.—Ruth 2:13, 17.

³⁰ Ruth's faith in action is an excellent example for all of us today who struggle in these difficult economic times. She did not think that others owed her anything, so she appreciated everything that was offered her. She felt no shame in working long and hard to care for one she loved, even though it was humble work. She gratefully accepted and applied wise advice about how to work safely and in good company. Most important, she never lost sight of where her true refuge lay—with her protective Father, Jehovah God.

³¹ If we show loyal love as Ruth did and follow her example in humility, industriousness, and appreciation, we will find that our faith too will become a helpful example for others. How, though, did Jehovah provide for Ruth and Naomi? We will discuss the matter in the following chapter.

28, 29. (a) What kind of reputation did Ruth have? (b) How can you, like Ruth, take refuge in Jehovah?

30, 31. What can we learn from Ruth about work habits, appreciation, and loyal love?

TO THINK ABOUT . . .

- How did Ruth express her faith in Jehovah God?
- How did Ruth show loyal love?
- Why did Jehovah value Ruth?
- In what ways would you like to imitate the faith of Ruth?

CHAPTER FIVE

"An Excellent Woman"

RUTH knelt by the pile of barley stalks she had gathered during the day. Evening was descending on the fields around Bethlehem, and many workers were already wending their way up to the gate of the little city perched atop a nearby ridge. Ruth's muscles surely protested the long day's labor, for she had been working steadily since the morning. Still she kept at it, swinging a small rod or flail down onto the stalks to loosen the grains. All in all, it had been a good day—better than she could ever have hoped for.

2 Were things finally starting to look up for this young widow? As we saw in the preceding chapter, she had attached herself to her mother-in-law, Naomi, vowing to stick with her and to make Naomi's God, Jehovah, her own God. Together the two bereaved women had come to Bethlehem from Moab, and Ruth the Moabitess soon learned that Jehovah's Law made practical, dignified provisions for the poor in Israel, including foreigners. And now she found that some of Jehovah's people, who lived under the Law and were trained by it, showed a degree of spirituality and kindness that touched her wounded heart.

3 One such person was Boaz, the wealthy older man in whose fields she was gleaning. He had taken fatherly notice of her today. She could not help but smile inwardly when she thought of his kind words praising her for caring for Naomi and for choosing to seek refuge under the wings of the true God, Jehovah. —*Read Ruth 2:11-14.*

4 Still, Ruth may have wondered about the life ahead of her. As an impoverished foreigner with neither husband nor child, how would she support herself and Naomi in the years ahead?

1, 2. (a) What kind of work was Ruth doing? (b) Ruth learned of what positive aspects of God's Law and his people?

3, 4. (a) How had Boaz encouraged Ruth? (b) How can Ruth's example help us in today's hard economic times?

Would gleaning suffice? And who would take care of *her* when she grew old? It would be understandable if such concerns weighed on her mind. In today's hard economic times, many struggle with similar anxieties. As we learn how Ruth's faith helped her through such challenges, we will find much to imitate.

What Makes a Family?

5 By the time Ruth finished beating out the grain and collecting it all together, she found that she had gleaned about an ephah measure, or 20 dry quarts, of barley. Her load may have weighed some 30 pounds! She hoisted it, perhaps bundling it in a cloth and carrying it on her head, and then made her way to Bethlehem in the gathering darkness.—Ruth 2:17.

6 Naomi was pleased to see her beloved daughter-in-law, and perhaps she gasped in surprise as she saw Ruth's heavy load of barley. Ruth also brought some food left over from the meal that Boaz had provided for the workers, and the two thus shared a simple meal. Naomi asked: "Where did you glean today, and where did you work? May the one who took notice of you become blessed." (Ruth 2:19) Naomi was attentive; she saw proof in Ruth's heavy load of provisions that someone had taken notice of the young widow and had treated her kindly.

7 The two fell to conversing, and Ruth told Naomi about the kindness of Boaz. Moved, Naomi replied: "Blessed be he of Jehovah, who has not left off his loving-kindness toward the living and the dead." (Ruth 2:20) She saw the kindness of Boaz as coming from Jehovah, who moves his servants to be generous and promises to reward his people for the kindness they show.*
—*Read Proverbs 19:17.*

8 Naomi urged Ruth to accept Boaz' offer to keep gleaning in his fields and to stay near the young women of his own household so that she would escape harassment from the reapers. Ruth took that advice. She also "kept on dwelling with her

---

* As Naomi noted, Jehovah's kindness is not restricted to the living; it even extends to the dead. Naomi had lost her husband and both sons. Ruth had lost her husband. Surely all three men had meant a great deal to both women. Any kindness shown to Naomi and Ruth was, in effect, kindness to the men who would have wanted those dear women to be cared for.

5, 6. (a) How successful was Ruth's first day of gleaning in the field of Boaz? (b) How did Naomi react when she saw Ruth?

7, 8. (a) Naomi saw the kindness of Boaz as coming from whom, and why? (b) How did Ruth further show her loyal love toward her mother-in-law?

mother-in-law." (Ruth 2:22, 23) In those words we see once more her hallmark quality—loyal love. Ruth's example may move us to ask ourselves whether we honor the bonds of family, loyally supporting our loved ones and offering them help as needed. Jehovah never fails to notice such loyal love.

⁹ Were Ruth and Naomi somehow less than a family? Some assume that there must be someone to fill each role—husband, wife, son, daughter, grandparent, and so forth—for a family to be "real." But the examples of Ruth and Naomi remind us that servants of Jehovah can open their hearts and make even the smallest of families glow with warmth, kindness, and love. Do you appreciate what family you have? Jesus reminded his followers that the Christian congregation can provide family even for those who have none.—Mark 10:29, 30.

"He Is One of Our Repurchasers"

¹⁰ From the barley harvest in April until the wheat harvest in June, Ruth kept gleaning in the fields of Boaz. As the weeks passed, Naomi no doubt thought more about what she could do for her beloved daughter-in-law. Back in Moab, Naomi had been convinced that she could never help Ruth find another husband. (Ruth 1: 11-13) Now, though, she was beginning to think differently. She approached Ruth and said: "My daughter, ought I not to look for a resting-place for you?" (Ruth 3:1) It was customary in those days for parents to find mates for their children, and Ruth had become a true daughter to Naomi. She wanted to find Ruth "a resting-place"—referring to the security and protection that a home and a husband might provide. But what could Naomi do?

> The examples of Ruth and Naomi remind us to appreciate what family we have

¹¹ When Ruth first mentioned Boaz, Naomi said: "The man is related to us. He is one of our repurchasers." (Ruth 2:20) What did that mean? God's Law to Israel included loving provisions for families who as a result of poverty or bereavement fell on

9. What can we learn from Ruth and Naomi about family?

10. In what way did Naomi want to help Ruth?

11, 12. (a) When Naomi called Boaz a "repurchaser," to what loving provision of God's Law was she referring? (b) How did Ruth respond to her mother-in-law's advice?

hard times. If a woman was widowed while still childless, she was especially devastated because her husband's name, his posterity, would be cut off, lost to future generations. However, God's Law allowed the man's brother to marry the widow so that she could give birth to an heir who might carry on her deceased husband's name and care for the family property.*—Deut. 25:5-7.

¹² Naomi related to Ruth a plan of action. We might imagine the young woman's eyes widening as her mother-in-law spoke. Israel's Law was still new to Ruth, and many of its customs were still quite foreign to her. Even so, she held Naomi in such high regard that she listened carefully to every word. What Naomi advised her to do might have seemed awkward or embarrassing—even potentially humiliating—yet Ruth agreed. She meekly said: "All that you say to me I shall do."—Ruth 3:5.

¹³ Sometimes it is difficult for young people to listen to the advice of those who are older and more experienced. It is easy to assume that older ones do not really understand the challenges and problems the young face. Ruth's humble example reminds us that listening to the wisdom of older ones who love us

---

* The right to marry such a widow was evidently extended first to the deceased man's brothers and then to the nearest male relatives, as was the right to inheritance.—Num. 27:5-11.

13. What lesson can we learn from Ruth about accepting advice from older ones? (See also Job 12:12.)

and have our best interests at heart can be very rewarding. (***Read Psalm 71:17, 18.***) But what was Naomi's advice, and was Ruth really rewarded for heeding it?

Ruth at the Threshing Floor

¹⁴ That evening, Ruth made her way to the threshing floor —a flat, hard-packed area where a number of farmers would take their grain for threshing and winnowing. The spot chosen was usually on a hillside or hilltop, where the breezes were strong in the late afternoon and early evening. To release the grain from the chaff and straw, workers used big forks or shovels to toss the mixture into the wind, which carried off the lighter chaff and allowed the heavier grains to fall back to the floor.

¹⁵ Ruth watched discreetly as the work wound down in the evening. Boaz oversaw the winnowing of his grain, which grew into a great heap. After eating heartily, he lay down at one end of the heap. This was evidently a common practice, perhaps designed to protect the precious harvest from thieves and marauders. Ruth saw Boaz settling down for the night. The time had come to put Naomi's plan into action.

¹⁶ Ruth crept closer, her heart racing. She could tell that the man was sound asleep. So just as Naomi had said, she went over to his feet, uncovered them, and lay down by them. Then she waited. The time passed. To Ruth, it must have felt like an eter-

---

14. What was a threshing floor, and how was it used?
15, 16. (a) Describe the scene at the threshing floor as Boaz finished working for the evening. (b) How did Boaz discover that Ruth was lying at his feet?

nity. Finally, around midnight, Boaz began to stir. Trembling from the cold, he stretched forward, likely to cover his feet up again. But he sensed that someone was there. As the account reads, "Look! a woman lying at his feet!"—Ruth 3:8.

¹⁷ "Who are you?" he asked. Ruth replied, perhaps with a tremor in her voice: "I am Ruth your slave girl, and you must spread out your skirt over your slave girl, for you are a repurchaser." (Ruth 3:9) Some modern interpreters have sought to imply that there were some sexual undertones in Ruth's actions and words, but they ignore two simple facts. First, Ruth was acting according to the customs of the day, many of which are long lost to us. So it would be a mistake to view her actions through the warped lens of today's debased moral standards. Second, Boaz responded in a way that clearly shows that he saw Ruth's conduct as morally chaste and highly commendable.

¹⁸ Boaz spoke, and no doubt his gentle, soothing tone comforted Ruth. He said: "Blessed may you be of Jehovah, my daughter. You have expressed your loving-kindness better in the last instance than in the first instance, in not going after the young fellows whether lowly or rich." (Ruth 3:10) "The first instance" referred to Ruth's loyal love in accompanying Naomi back to Israel and caring for her. "The last instance" was the present one. Boaz noted that a young woman like Ruth might easily have sought a husband among much younger men, whether rich or poor. Rather, she wanted to do good not only to Naomi but also to Naomi's deceased husband, to carry on the dead man's name in his homeland. It is not hard to see why Boaz was moved by this young woman's unselfishness.

> Because Ruth treated others with kindness and respect, she earned an excellent reputation

¹⁹ Boaz continued: "And now, my daughter, do not be afraid. All that you say I shall do for you, for everyone in the gate of my people is aware that you are an excellent woman." (Ruth 3: 11) He was pleased at the prospect of marrying Ruth; perhaps he

---

17. Those who imply that there was something improper in Ruth's actions ignore what two simple facts?

18. What did Boaz say to comfort Ruth, and to what two instances of her loving-kindness did he refer?

19, 20. (a) Why did Boaz not marry Ruth right away? (b) In what ways did Boaz show kindness and sensitivity toward Ruth and her reputation?

was not completely surprised to be asked to be her repurchaser. However, Boaz was a righteous man, and he was not about to act merely on his own preferences. He told Ruth that there was another repurchaser, one more closely related to the family of Naomi's dead husband. Boaz would approach that man first and give him the opportunity to become Ruth's husband.

20 Boaz urged Ruth to lie down again and rest until morning was near; then she could slip away unnoticed. He wanted to protect her reputation as well as his own, since people might wrongly assume that something immoral had taken place. Ruth lay near the man's feet again, perhaps with a mind more at ease after he had responded to her petition so kindly. Then, while it was still dark, she rose. Boaz filled her cloak with a generous gift of barley, and she made her way back into Bethlehem.—*Read Ruth 3:13-15.*

21 How satisfying it must have been for Ruth to contemplate what Boaz had said—that she was known among all the people as "an excellent woman"! No doubt her eagerness to get to know Jehovah and to serve him had much to do with that reputation. She had also shown great kindness and sensitivity toward Naomi and her people, willingly adapting to ways and customs that were surely unfamiliar to her. If we imitate Ruth's faith, we will seek to treat others and their ways and customs with deep respect. If we do, we too may find that we develop a reputation for excellence.

A Resting-Place for Ruth

22 "Who are you, my daughter?" Naomi said when Ruth arrived home. Perhaps it was the darkness that prompted the question, but Naomi also wanted to know whether Ruth was still the same unattached widow or one with prospects of marriage before her. Ruth quickly told her mother-in-law of all that had passed between her and Boaz. She also presented the generous gift of barley that Boaz had told her to give to Naomi.*—Ruth 3:16, 17.

---

* Boaz gave Ruth six measures of unspecified weight—perhaps to suggest that just as six work days were followed by a Sabbath rest, Ruth's own days of toil as a widow were soon to be followed by the "rest" that a secure home and a husband could provide. On the other hand, the six measures—perhaps shovelfuls—may simply have been all that Ruth could carry.

---

21. What contributed to Ruth's being known as "an excellent woman," and how can we imitate her example?

22, 23. (a) What may have been the meaning behind the gift that Boaz bestowed on Ruth? (See also footnote.) (b) What did Naomi urge Ruth to do?

Jehovah blessed Ruth with the privilege of becoming an ancestress of the Messiah

²³ Wisely, Naomi urged Ruth to sit at home quietly that day instead of going out to glean in the fields. She assured Ruth: "The man will have no rest unless he has brought the matter to an end today."—Ruth 3:18.

²⁴ Naomi was quite right about Boaz. He went to the city gate, where the city elders usually met, and waited until the man who was a closer relative passed by. In front of witnesses, Boaz offered the man the opportunity to act as repurchaser by marrying Ruth. However, the man refused, claiming that doing so would ruin his own inheritance. Then, before the witnesses there at the city gate, Boaz stated that he would act as the repurchaser, buying up the estate of Naomi's dead husband, Elimelech, and marrying Ruth, the widow of Elimelech's son Mahlon. Boaz declared his hope that doing so would "cause the name of the dead man to rise upon his inheritance." (Ruth 4:1-10) Boaz truly was an upright and unselfish man.

²⁵ Boaz married Ruth. Thereafter, we read: "Jehovah granted her conception and she bore a son." The women of Bethlehem blessed Naomi and praised Ruth for being better to Naomi than seven sons would have been. Later, we learn, Ruth's son became an ancestor of the great King David. (Ruth 4:11-22) David, in turn, was an ancestor of Jesus Christ.—Matt. 1:1.*

²⁶ Ruth was blessed indeed, as was Naomi, who helped to raise the child as if he were her own. The lives of these two women stand as vivid reminders that Jehovah God notices all those who toil humbly to provide for their own and who serve him loyally with his chosen people. He never fails to reward faithful people, such as Boaz, Naomi, and Ruth.

TO THINK ABOUT . . .

- How did Ruth show loyal love toward Naomi?

- How did Naomi show loyal love toward Ruth?

- Why does Jehovah treasure such servants as Boaz, Naomi, and Ruth?

- How do you hope to imitate the faith of Ruth?

---

* Ruth is one of five women whom the Bible lists in the ancestry of Jesus. Another one is Rahab, who was the mother of Boaz. (Matt. 1:3, 5, 6, 16) Like Ruth, she was not an Israelite.

24, 25. (a) How did Boaz show that he was an upright and unselfish man? (b) In what ways was Ruth blessed?

26. Of what do the examples of Ruth and Naomi remind us?

CHAPTER SIX

She Opened Her Heart to God in Prayer

HANNAH busied herself with preparations for the trip, trying to keep her mind occupied. It should have been a happy time; Elkanah, her husband, customarily took the whole family on these annual journeys to worship at the tabernacle in Shiloh. Jehovah meant for such occasions to be joyful. (***Read Deuteronomy 16: 15.***) And no doubt Hannah, from her childhood on, had delighted in those festivals. But things had changed for her in recent years.

² She was blessed to have a husband who loved her. However, Elkanah had another wife. Her name was Peninnah, and she seemed intent on making Hannah's life miserable. Peninnah had figured out a way to make even these annual occasions a source of acute pain for Hannah. How? More to the point, how did Hannah's faith in Jehovah help her to cope with what often seemed like an impossible situation? If you face challenges that sap you of joy in life, you may find Hannah's story particularly moving.

"Why Does Your Heart Feel Bad?"

³ The Bible reveals two big problems in Hannah's life. She had little control over the first and none at all over the second. In the first place, she was in a polygamous marriage, with a rival wife who hated her. In the second place, she was barren. That condition is difficult for any wife who longs to bear children; but in Hannah's time and culture, it was a source of intense grief. Each family counted on offspring to carry on the family name. Barrenness seemed a bitter reproach and shame.

⁴ Hannah might have borne her burden with fortitude had it not been for Peninnah. Polygamy was never an ideal situation. Rivalry, strife, and heartache were all too common. The practice

---

1, 2. (a) Why was Hannah unhappy when preparing for a trip? (b) What can we learn from Hannah's story?

3, 4. What two big problems did Hannah face, and why did each present a challenge?

was far from the standard of monogamy that God had set in the garden of Eden. (Gen. 2:24) The Bible thus paints a grim portrait of polygamy, and the poignant depiction of life within Elkanah's household is one of the telling brushstrokes in that picture.

⁵ Elkanah loved Hannah the most. Jewish tradition has it that he married Hannah first and that Peninnah came along some years later. At any rate, Peninnah, who was deeply jealous of Hannah, found many ways to make her rival suffer. Peninnah's great advantage over Hannah had to do with fertility. Peninnah produced one offspring after another, and her self-importance grew with each new child. Instead of feeling sorry for Hannah and comforting her in her disappointment, Peninnah played on that sensitive point. The Bible says that Peninnah vexed Hannah sorely "for the sake of making her feel disconcerted." (1 Sam. 1:6) Peninnah's actions were deliberate. She wanted to hurt Hannah, and she succeeded.

⁶ Peninnah's favorite opportunity, it seems, came at the time of the annual pilgrimage to Shiloh. To each of Peninnah's many children—"all her sons and her daughters"—Elkanah gave portions of the sacrifices offered to Jehovah. Childless Hannah, though, received only her own portion. Peninnah then so lorded it over Hannah and reminded her of her barrenness that the poor woman gave way to weeping and even lost her appetite. Elkanah could not help but notice that his beloved Hannah was distressed and was not eating, so he attempted to comfort her. "Hannah," he asked, "why do you weep, and why do you not eat, and why does your heart feel bad? Am I not better to you than ten sons?"—1 Sam. 1:4-8.

In the face of unkind treatment at home, Hannah turned to Jehovah for comfort

⁷ To his credit, Elkanah discerned that Hannah's distress had to do with her barrenness. And Hannah surely treasured his kind assurances of love.* But Elkanah did not mention Peninnah's malice; nor does the Bible record suggest

* Although the Bible record says that Jehovah had 'closed up Hannah's womb,' there is no evidence that God was displeased with this humble and faithful woman. (1 Sam. 1:5) The Bible at times attributes to God events that he simply allowed to take place for a time.

5. Why did Peninnah want Hannah to suffer, and how did she hurt Hannah?

6, 7. (a) Despite Elkanah's attempts to comfort Hannah, why might she have held back from telling him the whole story? (b) Did Hannah's barrenness mean that Jehovah was displeased with her? Explain. (See footnote.)

Hannah was deeply troubled by her barrenness, and Peninnah did everything she could to make Hannah feel worse

that Hannah told him of it. Perhaps she saw that exposing Peninnah would only make her own situation worse. Would Elkanah really change things? Might not Peninnah's contempt for Hannah only deepen, and would not the children and the servants of that spiteful woman follow suit? Hannah would only feel more and more like an outcast in her own household.

⁸ Whether Elkanah knew the full scope of Peninnah's petty meanness or not, Jehovah God saw it all. His Word reveals the whole picture, thus providing a solemn warning to any who indulge in seemingly minor jealous and hateful acts. On the other hand, the innocent and the peaceable, like Hannah, can find comfort in knowing that the God of justice sets all matters right in his own time and in his own way. (**Read Deuteronomy 32:4.**) Perhaps Hannah knew as much, for it was to Jehovah that she turned for help.

"Self-Concerned No More"

⁹ In the early hours, the household was bustling. Everyone was getting ready for the trip, even the children. The journey to Shiloh would take the large family across more than 20 miles of the hilly country of Ephraim.* The trek would last a day or two on foot. Hannah knew how her rival wife would act. However, Hannah did not stay at home. She thus set a worthy example for worshippers of God to this day. It is never wise to let the misconduct of others interfere with our worship of God. Were we to do so, we would miss out on the very blessings that strengthen us to endure.

¹⁰ After a long day of walking on winding mountain roads, the large family at last approached Shiloh. There it sat, on a hill nearly ringed by higher hills. As they approached, Hannah likely thought a great deal about what she would say in prayer to Jehovah. Once they arrived, the family shared a meal. Hannah pulled away from the group as soon as she could and made her way to the tabernacle of Jehovah. High Priest Eli was there, sitting near the doorpost. But Hannah's focus was on her God. Here at the

---

* The distance is based on the likelihood that Elkanah's hometown, Ramah, was the same place that came to be known as Arimathea in Jesus' day.

---

8. When you face petty meanness or injustice, why is it comforting to remember that Jehovah is the God of justice?

9. What lesson can we learn from Hannah's willingness to make the trip to Shiloh despite knowing how her rival would act?

10, 11. (a) Why did Hannah make her way to the tabernacle as soon as she could? (b) How did Hannah pour out her heart to her heavenly Father in prayer?

tabernacle, she felt confident that she would be heard. If no one else could fully understand her plight, her Father in heaven could. Her bitterness welled up within her, and she began to weep.

¹¹ As the sobs racked her body, Hannah spoke within herself to Jehovah. Her lips quivered as she mentally formed the words to express her pain. And she prayed at length, pouring out her heart to her Father. She did more, though, than just ask God to fulfill her desperate urge to bear offspring. Hannah was keen not only to receive blessings from God but also to give him what she could. So she made a vow, saying that if she had a son, she would dedicate the child to a life of service to Jehovah.—1 Sam. 1:9-11.

¹² Hannah thus set an example for all of God's servants when it comes to prayer. Jehovah kindly invites his people to speak to him openly, without reservation, pouring out their concerns before him as a trusting child would to a loving parent. (**Read Psalm 62:8; 1 Thessalonians 5:17.**) The apostle Peter was inspired to write these comforting words about prayer to Jehovah: "Throw all your anxiety upon him, because he cares for you."—1 Pet. 5:7.

¹³ Humans, however, are not as understanding and empathetic as Jehovah is. As Hannah wept and prayed, she was startled by a voice. It was Eli, the high priest, who had been observing her. He said: "How long will you behave drunk? Put away your wine from upon you." Eli had noticed Hannah's quivering lips, her sobs, and her emotional demeanor. Instead of inquiring what was wrong, he jumped to the conclusion that she was drunk.—1 Sam. 1:12-14.

¹⁴ How hurtful for Hannah, in that moment of anguish, to have to face such a baseless accusation—and that from a man who held such an honored position! Nevertheless, she again set a praiseworthy example of faith. She did not let a man's imperfections get in the way of her worship of Jehovah. She answered Eli respectfully and explained her situation. He replied, perhaps in a chastened and softer tone: "Go in peace, and may the God of Israel grant your petition that you have asked of him."—1 Sam. 1:15-17.

¹⁵ What was the effect on Hannah of opening her heart to

---

12. As Hannah's example illustrates, what should we keep in mind when it comes to prayer?

13, 14. (a) How did Eli jump to a wrong conclusion about Hannah? (b) How did Hannah's response to Eli set a remarkable example of faith?

15, 16. (a) How was Hannah affected by opening her heart to Jehovah and worshipping him at the tabernacle? (b) How might we follow Hannah's example when we struggle with negative feelings?

Jehovah and worshipping him there at his tabernacle? The account reads: "The woman proceeded to go on her way and to eat, and her face became self-concerned no more." (1 Sam. 1:18) *The Jerusalem Bible* here reads: "Her countenance was no more sad." Hannah felt relieved. She had, in a sense, transferred the weight of her emotional burden to shoulders infinitely broader and stronger than her own, those of her heavenly Father. (**Read Psalm 55:22.**) Is any problem too heavy for him? No—not then, not now, not ever!

¹⁶ When we feel loaded down, overwhelmed, or overcome with sadness, we do well to follow Hannah's example and speak openly to the One whom the Bible calls the "Hearer of prayer." (Ps. 65:2) If we do so in faith, we too may find that our sadness is replaced by "the peace of God that excels all thought."—Phil. 4:6, 7.

"There Is No Rock Like Our God"

¹⁷ The next morning, Hannah returned to the tabernacle with Elkanah. She had likely told him of her request and her commitment, for the Mosaic Law said that a husband had the right to nullify a vow made by his wife without his consent. (Num. 30:10-15) But that faithful man made no such move. Rather, he and Hannah worshipped Jehovah together at the tabernacle before heading homeward.

¹⁸ Just when did Peninnah realize that she had lost her power to upset Hannah? The account does not say, but the expression "self-concerned *no more*" suggests that Hannah's spirits rose from that time forward. At any rate, Peninnah soon found that her spiteful conduct produced no effect. The Bible never mentions her name again.

¹⁹ As the months passed, Hannah's peace of mind flowered into unbridled delight. She was pregnant! In her joy, Hannah never for a moment forgot where this blessing had come from. When the boy was born, she chose the name Samuel, which means "Name of God" and evidently refers to calling on the divine name, as Hannah had done. That year, she did not join Elkanah and the family for the trek to Shiloh. She stayed home with the child for three years, until he was weaned. Then she gathered her

---

17, 18. (a) How did Elkanah prove supportive regarding Hannah's vow? (b) What power over Hannah did Peninnah lose?

19. What blessing did Hannah receive, and how did she show that she appreciated where that blessing came from?

strength for the day on which she would have to part with her beloved son.

²⁰ The parting could not have been easy. Of course, Hannah knew that Samuel would be well cared for in Shiloh, perhaps by the hands of some of the women who served at the tabernacle. Still, he was so young, and what mother does not long to be with her child? Nonetheless, Hannah and Elkanah brought the boy, not begrudgingly, but gratefully. They offered sacrifices at God's house, and they presented Samuel to Eli, reminding him of the vow Hannah had made there years earlier.

²¹ Hannah then uttered a prayer that God deemed worthy of inclusion in his inspired Word. As you read her words, recorded at 1 Samuel 2:1-10, you will find the depth of her faith conveyed in every line. She praised Jehovah for his marvelous use of power—his unmatched ability to humble the haughty, to bless the oppressed, and to end life or even to save it from death. She praised her Father for his unique holiness, his justice, and his faithfulness. With good reason, Hannah could say: "There is no rock like our God." Jehovah is completely reliable and unchanging, a refuge for all the oppressed and downtrodden who turn to him for help.

²² Little Samuel was certainly privileged to have a mother who was so filled with faith in Jehovah. Though he surely missed her as he grew up, he never felt forgotten. Year after year, Hannah would

---

20. How did Hannah and Elkanah carry out the promise they had made to Jehovah?

21. How did Hannah's prayer to Jehovah reflect the depth of her faith? (See also the box "Two Remarkable Prayers.")

22, 23. (a) Why can we be sure that Samuel grew up knowing that his parents loved him? (b) How did Jehovah further bless Hannah?

Two Remarkable Prayers

Hannah's two prayers, recorded at 1 Samuel 1:11 and 2:1-10, contain a number of outstanding features. Consider just a few:

● Hannah addressed the first of the two prayers to "Jehovah of armies." She is the first person in the Bible record to be quoted as using that title. It occurs a total of 285 times in the Bible and refers to God's command over a vast array of spirit sons.

● Note that Hannah uttered the second prayer, not when her son was born, but when she and Elkanah offered him up for God's service at Shiloh. So Hannah's great joy lay, not in silencing her rival, Peninnah, but in being blessed by Jehovah.

● When Hannah said, "My horn is indeed exalted in Jehovah," she may have had in mind the ox, a powerful beast of burden that uses its horns mightily. Hannah was, in effect, saying: 'Jehovah, you make me strong.'—1 Sam. 2:1.

● Hannah's words about God's "anointed one" are considered prophetic. The expression is the same one rendered "messiah," and Hannah is the first person in the Bible record to use it to refer to a future anointed king.—1 Sam. 2:10.

● Jesus' mother, Mary, about 1,000 years later, echoed some of Hannah's expressions in her own words of praise to Jehovah.—Luke 1:46-55. (See Chapter 17.)

Hannah proved to be
a real blessing to her
son Samuel

TO THINK ABOUT . . .

- How did Hannah show faith despite opposition?
- How did Hannah's prayers reveal her faith?
- Why does Jehovah treasure such servants as Hannah?
- In what ways do you intend to imitate Hannah's faith?

come back to Shiloh, bringing a sleeveless coat for his service at the tabernacle. Every stitch bore evidence of her love and care for her son. (*Read 1 Samuel 2:19.*) We can just picture her putting the new coat on the boy, smoothing it out, and looking fondly at him while speaking kind, encouraging words. Samuel was blessed to have such a mother, and he grew up to be a blessing to his parents and to all of Israel.

23 As for Hannah, she was not forgotten either. Jehovah blessed her with fertility, and she bore Elkanah five more children. (1 Sam. 2:21) Perhaps Hannah's greatest blessing, though, was the bond between her and her Father, Jehovah, which grew ever stronger through the years. May the same happen to you, as you imitate the faith of Hannah.

CHAPTER SEVEN

He "Continued Growing Up With Jehovah"

SAMUEL looked into the faces of his people. The nation had gathered at the town of Gilgal, summoned by this faithful man who had served as prophet and judge for decades. It was May or June by modern reckoning; the dry season was well along. The fields in the region were golden with wheat ready for harvest. Silence fell over the crowd. How could Samuel reach their hearts?

² The people did not understand how serious their situation was. They had insisted on having a human king to rule over them. They did not grasp that they had shown gross disrespect to their God, Jehovah, and to his prophet. They were, in effect, rejecting Jehovah as their King! How could Samuel move them to repentance?

³ Samuel spoke. "I have grown old and gray," he told the crowd. His whitening hair added weight to his words. He then said: "I have walked before you from my youth until this day." (1 Sam. 11:14, 15; 12:2) Though Samuel was old, he had not forgotten his youth. His memories of those early days were still vivid. The decisions he had made back then, as a growing boy, had led him to a life of faith and devotion to his God, Jehovah.

⁴ Samuel had to build and maintain faith, although again and again he was surrounded by people who were faithless and disloyal. Today, it is just as challenging to build faith, for we live

> Samuel's boyhood can teach us much about building faith in Jehovah despite bad influences

---

1, 2. In what setting did Samuel address the people of Israel, and why did he need to move them to repentance?

3, 4. (a) Why did Samuel speak of his youth? (b) Why is Samuel's example of faith useful for us today?

in a faithless and corrupt world. (**Read Luke 18:8.**) Let us see what we can learn from Samuel's example, starting in his early boyhood.

"Ministering Before Jehovah, as a Boy"

⁵ Samuel had an unusual childhood. Shortly after he was weaned, at perhaps three years of age or a little more, he began a life of service at the sacred tabernacle of Jehovah at Shiloh, over 20 miles from his home in Ramah. His parents, Elkanah and Hannah, dedicated their boy to Jehovah in a special form of service, making him a lifelong Nazirite.* Did this mean that Samuel was cast off, unloved by his parents?

⁶ Far from it! They knew that their son would be cared for at Shiloh. High Priest Eli no doubt supervised matters, for Samuel worked closely with him. There were also a number of women who served in some connection with the tabernacle, evidently in an organized way.—Ex. 38:8; Judg. 11:34-40.

⁷ Furthermore, Hannah and Elkanah never forgot their beloved firstborn, whose very birth was an answer to a prayer. Hannah had asked God for a son, promising to dedicate the boy to God in a life of sacred service. When visiting each year, Hannah brought Samuel a new sleeveless coat she had made for his tabernacle service. The little boy surely cherished those visits. He no doubt thrived on his parents' loving encouragement and guidance as they taught him what a privilege it was to serve Jehovah in that unique place.

⁸ Parents today can learn a lot from Hannah and Elkanah. It is common for parents to focus all their childrearing efforts on material concerns while ignoring spiritual needs. But Samuel's parents put spiritual matters first, and that had a great bearing on the kind of man their son grew up to be.—*Read Proverbs 22:6.*

⁹ We can picture the boy growing bigger and exploring the hills around Shiloh. As he gazed down on the town and the val-

---

* Nazirites were under a vow that included a ban on drinking alcoholic beverages and on cutting their hair. Most undertook such vows for only a set period of time, but a few, such as Samson, Samuel, and John the Baptist, were lifelong Nazirites.

5, 6. How was Samuel's childhood unusual, but why were his parents sure that he was cared for?

7, 8. (a) Year by year, how did Samuel's parents give him loving encouragement? (b) What can parents today learn from Samuel's parents?

9, 10. (a) Describe the tabernacle and young Samuel's feelings about that sacred place. (See also footnote.) (b) What might Samuel's responsibilities have included, and how do you think young ones today might imitate his example?

ley that spread out below it on one side, his heart likely swelled with joy and pride when he caught sight of Jehovah's tabernacle. That tabernacle was a sacred place indeed.* Built nearly 400 years earlier under the direction of Moses himself, it was the one center for the pure worship of Jehovah in all the world.

¹⁰ Young Samuel grew to love the tabernacle. In the account he later wrote, we read: "Samuel was ministering before Jehovah, as a boy, having a linen ephod girded on." (1 Sam. 2:18) That simple sleeveless garment evidently indicated that Samuel assisted the priests at the tabernacle. Although not of the priestly class, Samuel had duties that included opening the doors to the tabernacle courtyard in the morning and attending to elderly Eli. As much as he enjoyed the privileges, though, in time his innocent heart became troubled. Something was terribly wrong at Jehovah's house.

Staying Pure in the Face of Corruption

¹¹ At a young age, Samuel witnessed genuine wickedness and corruption. Eli had two sons, named Hophni and Phinehas. Samuel's account reads: "The sons of Eli were good-for-nothing men; they did not acknowledge Jehovah." (1 Sam. 2: 12) The two thoughts in this verse go hand in hand. Hophni and Phinehas were "good-for-nothing men"—literally "sons of worthlessness"—because they had no regard for Jehovah. They thought nothing of his righteous standards and requirements. From that one failing sprang all their other sins.

Samuel must have been deeply troubled to see the wickedness of Eli's sons

¹² God's Law was specific about the priests' duties and the way that they were to offer sacrifices at his tabernacle. For good reason! Those sacrifices represented God's provisions to forgive sins so that people could be clean in his eyes, eligible for his blessing and guidance. But Hophni and

---

* The sanctuary was a rectangular structure, basically a great tent on a wooden framework. However, it was made of the finest of materials—sealskins, beautifully embroidered cloths, and costly woods plated with silver and gold. The sanctuary sat within a rectangular courtyard that included an impressive altar for sacrifices. Over time, other chambers evidently were erected at the sides of the tabernacle for the use of the priests. Samuel, it seems, slept in such a chamber.

11, 12. (a) Hophni and Phinehas manifested what principal failing? (b) What kind of wickedness and corruption did Hophni and Phinehas practice at the tabernacle? (See also footnote.)

Phinehas led their fellow priests to treat the offerings with great disrespect.*

13 Imagine young Samuel watching, wide-eyed, as such gross abuses went on uncorrected. How many people did he see—including poor, humble, downtrodden folk—approaching that sacred tabernacle in hopes of finding some spiritual comfort and strength, only to leave disappointed, hurt, or humiliated? And how did he feel when he learned that Hophni and Phinehas also disregarded Jehovah's laws on sexual morality, as they had relations with some of the women who were serving there at the tabernacle? (1 Sam. 2:22) Perhaps he looked hopefully to Eli to do something about it.

14 Eli was in the best position to address the growing disaster. As high priest, he was responsible for what took place at the tabernacle. As a father, he had an obligation to correct his sons. After all, they were hurting themselves as well as countless others in the land. However, Eli failed on both counts, as a father and as high priest. He offered his sons only a bland, weak scolding. (**Read 1 Samuel 2:23-25.**) But his sons needed far stronger discipline. They were committing sins worthy of death!

15 Matters reached such a point that Jehovah sent "a man of God," an unnamed prophet, to Eli with a strong message of judgment. Jehovah told Eli: "You keep honoring your sons more than me." God thus foretold that Eli's wicked sons would die on the same day and that Eli's family would suffer greatly, even losing its privileged position in the priestly class. Did this powerful warning bring about a change in that family? The record reveals no such change of heart.—1 Sam. 2:27–3:1.

16 How did all this corruption affect young Samuel? From time to time in this dark account, we find bright rays of light,

---

* The account provides two examples of disrespect. For one thing, the Law specified which pieces of a sacrificial offering were to go to the priests to eat. (Deut. 18:3) But at the tabernacle, the wicked priests had set up a very different practice. They would have their attendants simply jab a great fork into the cauldron where the meat was boiling, taking whatever choice morsel came out! For another thing, when people brought their sacrifices to be burned at the altar, the wicked priests would have an attendant bully the offerer, demanding the raw meat even before the fat of the sacrifice was offered to Jehovah.—Lev. 3:3-5; 1 Sam. 2:13-17.

13, 14. (a) How were sincere people no doubt affected by the wickedness at the tabernacle? (b) How did Eli fail, both as a father and as high priest?

15. Jehovah sent what strong message to Eli and how did Eli's family respond to the warning?

16. (a) What reports do we read regarding young Samuel's progress? (b) Do you find those reports heartwarming? Explain.

Isa 2:18

Despite his fear, Samuel faithfully relayed Jehovah's judgment message to Eli

good news about Samuel's growth and progress. Recall that at 1 Samuel 2:18, we read that Samuel was faithfully "ministering before Jehovah, as a boy." Even at that early age, Samuel centered his life on his service to God. In verse 21 of the same chapter, we read something even more heartwarming: "The boy Samuel continued growing up with Jehovah." As he grew, his bond with his heavenly Father got stronger. Such a close personal relationship with Jehovah is the surest protection against any form of corruption.

¹⁷ It would have been easy for Samuel to reason that if the high priest and his sons can give in to sin, he might as well do whatever he wished. But the corruption of others, including those in positions of authority, is never an excuse to sin. Today, many Christian youths follow Samuel's example and keep "growing up with Jehovah"—even when some around them fail to set a good example.

¹⁸ How did such a course work out for Samuel? We read: "All the while the boy Samuel was growing bigger and more likable both from Jehovah's standpoint and from that of men." (1 Sam. 2:26) So Samuel was well-liked, at least by those whose opinions mattered. Jehovah himself cherished this boy for his faithful course. And Samuel surely knew that his God would act against all the badness going on in Shiloh, but perhaps he wondered when. One night, such questions met an answer.

17, 18. (a) How might Christian youths imitate Samuel's example when faced with corruption? (b) What shows that Samuel chose the right course?

"Speak, for Your Servant Is Listening"

19 It was nearing morning but still dark; the flickering light of the tent's great lamp was still burning. In the stillness, Samuel heard a voice calling his name. He thought it was Eli, who was now very old and nearly blind. Samuel got up and "went running" to the old man. Can you see the boy in your mind's eye, hurrying barefoot to see what Eli needed? It is touching to note that Samuel treated Eli with respect and kindness. In spite of all his sins, Eli was still Jehovah's high priest.—1 Sam. 3:2-5.

20 Samuel woke Eli, saying: "Here I am, for you called me." But Eli said that he had not called and sent the boy back to bed. Well, the same thing happened again and then again! Finally, Eli realized what was going on. It had become rare for Jehovah to send a vision or a prophetic message to his people, and it is not hard to see why. But Eli knew that Jehovah was speaking again—now to this boy! Eli told Samuel to go back to bed and instructed him on how to answer properly. Samuel obeyed. Soon he heard the voice calling: "Samuel, Samuel!" The boy answered: "Speak, for your servant is listening."—1 Sam. 3:1, 5-10.

21 Jehovah did, at last, have a servant in Shiloh who was listening. That became Samuel's life pattern. Is it yours? We do not have to wait for a supernatural voice in the night to speak to us. Today, God's voice is always there for us in a sense. It is there in his completed Word, the Bible. The more we listen to God and respond, the more our faith will grow. So it was with Samuel.

22 That night in Shiloh was a milestone in Samuel's life, for then he began to know Jehovah in a special sense, becoming God's own prophet and spokesman. At first, the boy was afraid to deliver Jehovah's message to Eli, for it was a final pronouncement that the prophecy against that family was soon to come true. But Samuel mustered the courage—and Eli humbly acquiesced to the divine judgment. Before long, everything Jehovah had said was fulfilled: Israel went to war with the Philistines, Hophni and Phinehas were both killed on the same day, and Eli

19, 20. (a) Describe what happened to Samuel late one night at the tabernacle. (b) How did Samuel learn the source of the message, and how did he treat Eli?

21. How can we listen to Jehovah today, and why is it worthwhile to do so?

22, 23. (a) How did the message that Samuel at first feared to deliver come true? (b) How did Samuel's reputation continue to grow?

Samuel prayed in faith, and Jehovah answered with a thunderstorm

himself died on learning that Jehovah's sacred Ark had been captured.—1 Sam. 3:10-18; 4:1-18.

23 However, Samuel's reputation as a faithful prophet only grew. "Jehovah himself proved to be with him," the account says, adding that Jehovah let none of Samuel's prophecies fail. —*Read 1 Samuel 3:19.*

Move forward in time → ## "Samuel Called to Jehovah"

24 Did the Israelites follow Samuel's lead and become spiritual, faithful people? No. In time, they decided that they did not want a mere prophet to judge them. They wanted to be like other nations and have a human king rule over them. At Jehovah's direction, Samuel complied. But he had to convey to Israel the magnitude of their sin. They were rejecting, not a mere man, but Jehovah himself! So he summoned the people to Gilgal.

25 Let us rejoin him in that tense moment of addressing Israel at Gilgal. There, elderly Samuel reminded Israel of his faithful record of integrity. Then, we read: "Samuel called to Jehovah." He asked Jehovah for a thunderstorm.—1 Sam. 12:17, 18.

26 A thunderstorm? In the dry season? Why, such a thing was unheard of! If there was even a trace of skepticism or scoffing among the people, it did not last long. The sky suddenly darkened with clouds. The winds battered the wheat in the fields. The thunder let out its booming, deafening roars. And the rain fell. The response? "The people were greatly in fear of Jehovah and of Samuel." At last, they saw how seriously they had sinned. —1 Sam. 12:18, 19.

27 Not Samuel, but his God, Jehovah, had reached their rebellious hearts. From his youth to his old age, Samuel put faith in his God. And Jehovah rewarded him. To this day, Jehovah has not changed. He still supports those who imitate the faith of Samuel.

TO THINK ABOUT . . .

- What helped Samuel's faith to grow during his youth?
- How did Samuel's faith enable him to resist bad influences?
- How did Samuel's faith help him to overcome fear?
- What are some ways that you would like to imitate the faith of Samuel?

24. In time, what decision did the Israelites make, and why was that a serious sin?

25, 26. At Gilgal, how did elderly Samuel finally help his people to see the seriousness of their sin against Jehovah?

27. How does Jehovah feel about those who imitate the faith of Samuel?

CHAPTER EIGHT

He Endured Despite Disappointments

SAMUEL could feel the grief in Shiloh. It almost seemed that the town was awash in tears. From how many houses did the cries of women and children emanate, the sounds of grieving over the news about fathers, husbands, sons, and brothers who would not be coming home? We know only that Israel had lost some 30,-000 soldiers in a terrible defeat at the hands of the Philistines not long after the loss of 4,000 in another battle.—1 Sam. 4:1, 2, 10.

2 That was just part of a string of tragedies. High Priest Eli's two wicked sons, Hophni and Phinehas, had marched out of Shiloh with the sacred ark of the covenant. Usually housed in the holy compartment of the tabernacle—a tentlike temple—this precious chest was a symbol of God's presence. The people then took the Ark into battle, foolishly thinking that it would act as a talisman and give them victory. But the Philistines captured the Ark, killing Hophni and Phinehas.—1 Sam. 4:3-11.

3 The tabernacle in Shiloh had been honored with the presence of the Ark for centuries. Now it was gone. Upon hearing this news, 98-year-old Eli fell backward from his seat and died. His daughter-in-law, widowed that very day, died in childbirth. Before expiring, she said: "Glory has gone away from Israel into exile." Indeed, Shiloh would never be the same.—1 Sam. 4:12-22.

4 How would Samuel cope with these profound disappointments? Would his faith stand up to the challenge of helping a people who had lost Jehovah's protection and favor? All of us today may, at times, face hardships and disappointments that challenge our faith, so let us see what more we can learn from Samuel.

---

1. Why was Shiloh full of grief and mourning?

2, 3. What string of tragedies had brought shame and loss of glory to Shiloh?

4. What will we discuss in this chapter?

How could Samuel help his people cope with terrible loss and disappointment?

He "Effected Righteousness"

5 The Bible record turns away from Samuel at this point and follows the sacred Ark, showing us how the Philistines suffered for taking it and were forced to return it. When we again come upon Samuel, some 20 years have passed. (1 Sam. 7:2) How was he occupied during those years? We need not guess.

6 We learn that before this period began, "the word of Samuel *continued* to come to all Israel." (1 Sam. 4:1) The record reveals that after the period was over, Samuel made a custom of visiting three cities in Israel, making a circuit each year, handling disputes and resolving questions. Then he would return to his hometown of Ramah. (1 Sam. 7:15-17) Clearly, Samuel always kept busy, and during that 20-year interval, he had much to do.

7 The immorality and corruption of Eli's sons had eroded the people's faith. Many, it seems, turned to idolatry as a result. After two decades of hard work, though, Samuel delivered this message to the people: "If it is with all your heart you are returning to Jehovah, put away the foreign gods from your midst and also the Ashtoreth images, and direct your heart unswervingly to Jehovah and serve him alone, and he will deliver you from the hand of the Philistines."—1 Sam. 7:3.

Though the Bible record contains no mention of Samuel for a 20-year period, we can be sure that he kept busy in Jehovah's service

8 "The hand of the Philistines" had grown heavy on the people. With Israel's army effectively smashed, the Philistines felt that they could oppress God's people with impunity. But Samuel assured the people that things would change if only they returned to Jehovah. Were they willing? To Samuel's delight, they put away their idols and "began serving Jehovah alone." Samuel convened an assembly at Mizpah, a town in the mountainous country north of Jerusalem. The people gathered, fasted, and repented for their many sins of idolatry.—*Read 1 Samuel 7:4-6.*

9 However, the Philistines learned of this great gathering and

---

5, 6. What does the Bible record focus on regarding a 20-year period, and how was Samuel occupied during that time?

7, 8. (a) What message did Samuel deliver to the people after two decades of hard work? (b) How did the people respond to Samuel's assurance?

9. The Philistines saw what opportunity, and how did God's people respond to the danger?

saw an opportunity. They sent their army to Mizpah to crush those worshippers of Jehovah. The Israelites heard news of the approaching danger. Terrified, they asked Samuel to pray for them. He did so, offering a sacrifice as well. During that sacred ceremony, the Philistine army came up against Mizpah. Jehovah then answered Samuel's prayer. In effect, Jehovah let out a roar of indignation. He "caused it to thunder with a loud noise on that day against the Philistines."—1 Sam. 7:7-10.

¹⁰ Now, should we imagine that those Philistines were like little children who scurry in fear to hide behind their mothers when they hear a thunderclap? No, these were tough, battle-hardened soldiers. This thunder, then, must have been unlike anything they knew. Was it the sheer volume of this "loud noise"? Did it come out of a clear blue sky, or did it echo bafflingly from the hillsides? At any rate, it shook those Philistines to the core. In utter confusion, they changed quickly from bullies to targets. The men of Israel poured forth from Mizpah, defeated them, and chased them for miles, to a place southwest of Jerusalem.—1 Sam. 7:11.

The Philistines thought that a gathering of Jehovah's repentant people was an opportunity to oppress them

¹¹ That battle was a turning point. The Philistines kept retreating during the rest of Samuel's days as judge. City after city returned to the control of God's people.—1 Sam. 7:13, 14.

¹² Many centuries later, the apostle Paul listed Samuel among the faithful judges and prophets who "effected righteousness." (Heb. 11:32, 33) Samuel did indeed help to bring about what was good and right in God's eyes. He remained effective because he waited patiently on Jehovah, faithfully keeping at his work in spite of disappointments. He also showed an appreciative spirit. After the victory at Mizpah, Samuel had a monument erected to commemorate the way that Jehovah had helped his people.—1 Sam. 7:12.

¹³ Do you want to 'effect righteousness'? If so, you do well

10, 11. (a) Why must there have been something unusual about the thunder that Jehovah directed against the Philistine army? (b) What resulted from the battle that began at Mizpah?
12. What does it mean that Samuel "effected righteousness," and what qualities helped him to remain effective?
13. (a) What qualities do we need if we are to imitate Samuel? (b) When do you think is a good time to develop traits like those of Samuel?

to learn from Samuel's patience and his humble, appreciative spirit. (*Read 1 Peter 5:6.*) Who of us does not need those qualities? It was good for Samuel to acquire and display such traits when relatively young, for he faced deeper disappointments in his later years.

"Your Own Sons Have Not Walked in Your Ways"

¹⁴ The next time we see Samuel, he "had grown old." Samuel had two adult sons by this time, Joel and Abijah, and he entrusted them with the responsibility of helping him in the work of judging. Sadly, though, his trust was misplaced. Honest and righteous though Samuel was, his sons used their positions for selfish ends, perverting justice and taking bribes.—1 Sam. 8:1-3.

¹⁵ One day, the older men of Israel approached the elderly prophet to complain. "Your own sons have not walked in your ways," they said. (1 Sam. 8:4, 5) Was Samuel aware of the problem? The account does not say. Unlike Eli, however, Samuel was

How did Samuel cope with the disappointment of having sons who went bad?

14, 15. (a) What severe disappointment did Samuel face after he "had grown old"? (b) Was Samuel a reprehensible father in the manner of Eli? Explain.

surely not a reprehensible father. Jehovah had rebuked and punished Eli for failing to correct his sons' wickedness, for honoring his sons more than God. (1 Sam. 2:27-29) Jehovah never found such fault with Samuel.

16 The account does not reveal Samuel's agonizing shame, anxiety, or disappointment once he learned of his sons' wicked conduct. Many parents, however, can imagine his feelings only too well. In today's dark times, rebellion against parental authority and discipline is pandemic. (*Read 2 Timothy 3:1-5.*) Parents who are dealing with that kind of pain may find a measure of comfort and guidance in Samuel's example. He did not let his sons' faithless ways alter his own course one bit. Remember, even after words and discipline fail to reach hardened hearts, parental example remains a powerful teacher. And parents always have the opportunity to make their own Father, Jehovah God, proud —as did Samuel.

"Do Appoint for Us a King"

17 Samuel's sons could not have imagined how far the effects of their greed and selfishness would reach. The older men of Israel went on to say to Samuel: "Now do appoint for us a king to judge us like all the nations." Did that demand feel like a rejection to Samuel? After all, he had been judging those people on Jehovah's behalf for decades. Now they wanted, not some mere prophet like Samuel, but a king to be their judge. The nations round about had kings, and the Israelites wanted one too! How did Samuel react? We read that "the thing was bad in the eyes of Samuel."—1 Sam. 8:5, 6.

18 Note how Jehovah responded when Samuel took the matter to him in prayer: "Listen to the voice of the people as respects all that they say to you; for it is not you whom they have rejected, but it is I whom they have rejected from being king over them." How comforting for Samuel, yet how awful an insult those people had flung at Almighty God! Jehovah told his prophet to warn the Israelites of the high price they would pay for having a human king. When Samuel complied, they insisted: "No,

---

16. What feelings afflict parents of rebellious children, and how might parents find a measure of comfort and guidance in Samuel's example?
17. What did the older men of Israel demand of Samuel, and how did he react?
18. How did Jehovah comfort Samuel and yet reveal the seriousness of Israel's sin?

but a king is what will come to be over us." Ever obedient to his God, Samuel went and anointed the king whom Jehovah chose. —1 Sam. 8:7-19.

19 How, though, did Samuel obey? In a resentful, perfunctory way? Did he allow disappointment to poison his heart, letting bitterness take root? Many a man might respond that way in such a situation, but not Samuel. He anointed Saul and acknowledged that the man was Jehovah's own choice. He kissed Saul, a sign of welcome and submission to the new king. And he said to the people: "Have you seen the one whom Jehovah has chosen, that there is none like him among all the people?"—1 Sam. 10: 1, 24.

20 Samuel focused, not on faults, but on the good in the man whom Jehovah had chosen. As for himself, he focused on his own record of integrity to God rather than on the approval of fickle people. (1 Sam. 12:1-4) He also worked faithfully at his own assignment, counseling God's people about the spiritual dangers they faced and encouraging them to remain faithful to Jehovah. His counsel reached their hearts, and the people begged Samuel to pray in their behalf. He gave them this beautiful reply: "It is unthinkable, on my part, to sin against Jehovah by ceasing to pray in your behalf; and I must instruct you in the good and right way."—1 Sam. 12:21-24.

> Samuel's example reminds us never to let jealousy or bitterness take root in our heart

21 Have you ever felt disappointed when someone else was chosen for a certain position or privilege? Samuel's example is a powerful reminder that we must never let jealousy or bitterness take root in our heart. (**Read Proverbs 14:30.**) God has plenty of rewarding, fulfilling work for each of his faithful servants.

"For How Long Will You Be Mourning for Saul?"

22 Samuel was right to see good in Saul; this was a remarkable man. Tall and impressive in appearance, he was courageous

19, 20. (a) In what ways did Samuel obey Jehovah's direction to anoint Saul as king of Israel? (b) How did Samuel continue to help Jehovah's people?

21. How might Samuel's example prove helpful if you ever feel disappointed when someone else receives a position or privilege?

22. Why was Samuel right to see good in Saul initially?

and resourceful yet initially modest and unassuming. (1 Sam. 10: 22, 23, 27) In addition to such gifts, he had a precious one—free will, the ability to choose his life course and make his own decisions. (Deut. 30:19) Did he use that gift well?

23 Sadly, when a man basks in the warm glow of newly acquired power, modesty is often the first quality to melt away. Before long, Saul began to turn arrogant. He chose to disobey Jehovah's orders that Samuel transmitted to him. Once, Saul grew impatient and offered up a sacrifice that Samuel intended to offer. Samuel had to give him strong correction and foretold that the kingship would not remain in Saul's family. Instead of being chastened by the discipline, Saul went on to commit worse acts of disobedience.—1 Sam. 13:8, 9, 13, 14.

24 Through Samuel, Jehovah told Saul to wage war against the Amalekites. Jehovah's instructions included an order to execute their wicked king, Agag. However, Saul spared Agag as well as the best of the spoil, which was to be destroyed. When Samuel came to correct him, Saul revealed how much he had changed. Instead of modestly accepting correction, he rationalized, excused himself, justified his actions, sidestepped the issue, and tried to shift the blame to the people. When Saul tried to deflect the discipline by claiming that some of the spoil was intended for a sacrifice to Jehovah, Samuel uttered the famous words: "Look! To obey is better than a sacrifice." Courageously, Samuel rebuked the man and revealed Jehovah's decision: The kingship would be ripped away from Saul and given to another—a better man.*—1 Sam. 15:1-33.

> Samuel learned that no disappointment is too great for Jehovah to heal, to resolve, or even to turn into a blessing

25 Samuel was deeply upset over Saul's failings. He spent the

---

* Samuel himself executed Agag. Neither that wicked king nor his family deserved leniency. Centuries later, Agag's descendants evidently included "Haman the Agagite," who attempted to wipe out all of God's people.—Esther 8:3; see Chapters 15 and 16 of this publication.

---

23. What precious quality did Saul lose first, and how did he show his growing arrogance?

24. (a) How did Saul disobey Jehovah in the war against the Amalekites? (b) How did Saul respond to correction, and what was Jehovah's decision?

25, 26. (a) Why did Samuel mourn for Saul, and how did Jehovah gently reprove His prophet? (b) What lesson did Samuel learn when he went to the house of Jesse?

night crying out to Jehovah about the matter. He even went into mourning for the man. Samuel had seen so much potential in Saul, so much good, and now such hopes were shattered. The man he once knew had changed—he had lost his best qualities and turned against Jehovah. Samuel refused to see Saul ever again. In time, though, Jehovah offered Samuel this gentle reproof: "For how long will you be mourning for Saul, while I, on the other hand, have rejected him from ruling as king over Israel? Fill your horn with oil and go. I shall send you to Jesse the Bethlehemite, because I have provided among his sons a king for myself."—1 Sam. 15:34, 35; 16:1.

26 Jehovah's purpose does not depend on the wavering loyalties of imperfect humans. If one man turns unfaithful, Jehovah will find another to carry out His will. So aged Samuel let go of his grief over Saul. At Jehovah's direction, Samuel went to the home of Jesse in Bethlehem, where he met a number of Jesse's impressive-looking sons. Yet, from the first, Jehovah reminded Samuel to look beyond mere physical attributes. (*Read 1 Samuel 16:7.*) Finally, Samuel met the youngest son, and here was Jehovah's choice—David!

27 In his final years, Samuel got to see ever more clearly the rightness of Jehovah's decision to replace Saul with David. Saul descended into murderous jealousy and apostasy. David, however, showed beautiful qualities—courage, integrity, faith, and loyalty. As Samuel's life drew to a close, his faith grew ever stronger. He saw that no disappointment is too great for Jehovah to heal, to resolve, or even to turn into a blessing. Finally, Samuel died, leaving behind the record of a remarkable life that spanned the better part of a century. All of Israel mourned the loss of that faithful man—and no wonder! To this day, servants of Jehovah do well to ask, 'Will I imitate the faith of Samuel?'

TO THINK ABOUT . . .

- How did Samuel cope with the tragedies that befell Shiloh?

- What enabled Samuel to endure despite the rebellion of his sons?

- How did Samuel recover from disappointments regarding King Saul?

- In what ways would you like to imitate the faith of Samuel?

---

27. (a) What helped Samuel's faith to keep growing stronger? (b) How do you feel about the example that Samuel set?

CHAPTER NINE

She Acted With Discretion

ABIGAIL saw the panic in the young man's eyes. He was terrified —and for good reason. Grave danger loomed. Right at that moment, some 400 warriors were on the way, determined to kill off every male in the household of Nabal, Abigail's husband. Why?

2 It had all started with Nabal. He had acted cruelly and insolently, as usual. This time, though, he had insulted the wrong man—the beloved commander of a loyal and well-trained band of warriors. Now, one of Nabal's young workmen, perhaps a shepherd, came to Abigail, trusting that she would come up with a plan to save them. But what could one woman do against an army?

> What could one woman do against an army?

3 First, let us learn a little more about this remarkable woman. Who was Abigail? How had this crisis arisen? And what can we learn from her example of faith?

"Good in Discretion and Beautiful in Form"

4 Abigail and Nabal were not a good match. Nabal could hardly have chosen a better spouse, whereas Abigail found herself married to one who could hardly have been worse. Granted, the man had money. He thus saw himself as very important, but how did others view him? It would be difficult to find a Bible character who is spoken of in more contemptuous terms. His very name means "Senseless," or "Stupid." Did his parents give him such a name at birth, or was it an epithet that stuck to him later? In either case, he lived up to his name. Nabal was "harsh

---

1-3. (a) How did danger come to loom over Abigail's household? (b) What will we learn about this remarkable woman?

4. What kind of man was Nabal?

and bad in his practices." A bully and a drunkard, he was widely feared and disliked.—1 Sam. 25:2, 3, 17, 21, 25.

5 Abigail was altogether different from Nabal. Her name means "My Father Has Made Himself Joyful." Many a father is proud to have a beautiful daughter, but a wise father is far happier to discern inner beauty in his child. All too often, a person blessed with outward beauty fails to see the need to develop such qualities as discretion, wisdom, courage, or faith. Not so with Abigail. The Bible praises her for her discretion as well as for her beauty.—*Read 1 Samuel 25:3.*

6 Some today might wonder why such an intelligent young woman married such a good-for-nothing man. Remember, many marriages in Bible times were arranged. If not, parental consent was still of great importance. Did Abigail's parents favor this marriage, even arrange it, because they were impressed with Nabal's wealth and prominence? Did they feel pressured by poverty? At any rate, Nabal's money did not make him a fit husband.

7 Wise parents carefully teach their children a wholesome view of marriage. They neither urge their children to marry for money nor pressure them to begin dating when still too young to take on adult roles and responsibilities. (1 Cor. 7:36) However, it was too late for Abigail to think about such things. For whatever reason, she was married to Nabal, and she was determined to make the best of a difficult situation.

"He Screamed Rebukes at Them"

8 Nabal had just made Abigail's situation harder than ever. The man he had insulted was none other than David. This was the faithful servant of Jehovah whom Samuel the prophet had anointed, revealing David as God's choice to succeed Saul as king. (1 Sam. 16:1, 2, 11-13) On the run from the jealous and murderous King Saul, David was dwelling in the wilderness with his 600 loyal warriors.

9 Nabal lived in Maon but worked and likely owned land in

5, 6. (a) What do you think were Abigail's most appealing qualities? (b) Why might Abigail have married such a good-for-nothing man?

7. (a) What should parents today avoid if they want to teach their children a wholesome view of marriage? (b) What was Abigail determined to do?

8. Whom had Nabal insulted, and why would you say that this was most unwise?

9, 10. (a) David and his men were struggling to survive in what setting? (b) Why should Nabal have appreciated what David and his men had been doing? (See also paragraph 10 footnote.)

77

nearby Carmel.* Those towns lay amidst grassy uplands suitable for raising sheep, of which Nabal owned 3,000. All around, though, was wild country. To the south lay the vast wilderness of Paran. To the east, the approach to the Salt Sea led through desolate wastelands riddled with ravines and caves. In these regions David and his men struggled to survive, no doubt hunting for their food and enduring many hardships. They often encountered the young men who worked as shepherds for the wealthy Nabal.

10 How did those hardworking soldiers treat the shepherds? It would have been easy for them to help themselves to a sheep now and then, but they did nothing of the kind. On the contrary, they were like a protective wall around Nabal's flocks and servants. (*Read 1 Samuel 25:15, 16.*) Sheep and shepherds faced plenty of dangers. Predators abounded, and Israel's southern border was so close that bands of foreign marauders and thieves frequently attacked.#

11 It must have been quite an undertaking to keep all those men fed in the wilderness. So one day David sent ten messengers to Nabal to ask for help. David chose the moment wisely. It was the festive time of sheepshearing, when generosity and feasting were customary. David also chose his words with care, using polite terms and forms of address. He even referred to himself as "your son David," perhaps a respectful acknowledgment of Nabal's greater age. How did Nabal respond?—1 Sam. 25:5-8.

12 He was outraged! "He screamed rebukes at them" is how the young man mentioned at the outset described the scene to Abigail. Miserly Nabal complained loudly about his precious bread, water, and slaughtered meat. He ridiculed David as inconsequential and compared him to a runaway servant. Nabal's view may have been similar to that of Saul, who hated David. Neither man had Jehovah's view. God loved David and saw him, not as a rebellious slave, but as the future king of Israel.—1 Sam. 25:10, 11, 14.

---

* This was not the famous Mount Carmel far to the north where the prophet Elijah later had a showdown with the prophets of Baal. (See Chapter 10.) This Carmel was a town at the edge of the southern wilderness.

David likely felt that protecting the local landowners and their flocks was a service to Jehovah God. In those days, it was Jehovah's purpose for the descendants of Abraham, Isaac, and Jacob to dwell in that land. Protecting it from foreign invaders and marauding bands was thus a form of sacred service.

11, 12. (a) How did David show tact and respect in his message to Nabal? (b) What was wrong with the way Nabal responded to David's message?

¹³ When the emissaries reported back to David, he became furious. "Gird on every one his sword!" he commanded. Arming himself, David led 400 of his men to attack. He vowed to wipe out every male in Nabal's household. (1 Sam. 25:12, 13, 21, 22) David's ire was understandable, but his way of expressing it was wrong. The Bible says: "Man's wrath does not work out God's righteousness." (Jas. 1:20) How, though, could Abigail save her household?

"Blessed Be Your Sensibleness"

¹⁴ In a way, we have already seen Abigail take the first step toward righting this terrible wrong. Unlike her husband, Nabal, she proved willing to listen. As for bringing the matter to Nabal, the young servant said of him: "He is too much of a good-for-nothing fellow to speak to him."* (1 Sam. 25:17) Tragically, Nabal's view of his own importance rendered him unwilling to listen. Such arrogance is all too common even to this day. But the young man knew Abigail to be different, which is no doubt why he approached her with this problem.

Unlike Nabal, Abigail proved willing to listen

¹⁵ Abigail thought and acted quickly. "At once Abigail hastened," we read. Four times in this one account we find the same verb, "to hasten," used regarding this woman. She prepared a generous gift for David and his men. It included bread, wine, sheep, roasted grain, cakes of raisins, and cakes of figs. Clearly, Abigail knew well what she had and was thoroughly in charge of her household responsibilities, much like the capable wife later described in the book of Proverbs. (Prov. 31:10-31) She sent the provisions ahead with some of her servants, then followed alone. "But," we read, "to her husband Nabal she told nothing." —1 Sam. 25:18, 19.

---

* The phrase the young man used literally means "a son of belial (worthlessness)." Other Bible renderings of this sentence include a description of Nabal as a man "who won't listen to anyone" and the conclusion, "it is no good talking to him."

---

13. (a) How did David initially respond to Nabal's insult? (b) What light does the principle recorded at James 1:20 shed on David's reaction?

14. (a) In what way did Abigail take the first step toward righting the wrong that Nabal had committed? (b) What practical lesson might we learn from the contrast between Nabal and Abigail? (See also footnote.)

15, 16. (a) How did Abigail show that she was like the capable wife described in the book of Proverbs? (b) Why was Abigail's course not a case of rebelling against her husband's rightful headship?

16 Does this mean that Abigail was rebelling against her husband's rightful headship? No; keep in mind that Nabal had acted wickedly against an anointed servant of Jehovah, an action that could well result in death for many innocent members of Nabal's household. If Abigail failed to act, might she become a sharer in her husband's guilt? In this case, she had to put submission to her God ahead of submission to her husband.

17 Before long, Abigail met up with David and his men. Again she hastened, this time to descend from her donkey and humble herself before David. (1 Sam. 25:20, 23) Then she poured out her heart at length, making a powerful plea for mercy in behalf of her husband and her household. What made her words effective?

18 She took responsibility for the problem and asked David to forgive her personally. She realistically acknowledged that her husband was as senseless as his name implied, perhaps suggesting that it would be beneath David's dignity to chastise such a man. She expressed her trust in David as Jehovah's representative, recognizing that he was fighting "the wars of Jehovah." She also indicated that she knew of Jehovah's promise regarding David and the kingship, for she said: "Jehovah . . . certainly will commission you as leader over Israel." Further, she urged David not to take any action that might bring bloodguilt upon him or that might later become "a cause for staggering"—evidently referring to a troubled conscience. (**Read 1 Samuel 25:24-31.**) Kind, moving words!

19 And how did David respond? He accepted what Abigail had brought and said: "Blessed be Jehovah the God of Israel, who has sent you this day to meet me! And blessed be your sensibleness, and blessed be you who have restrained me this day from entering into bloodguilt." David praised her for bravely hastening to meet him, and he acknowledged that she had restrained him from incurring bloodguilt. "Go up in peace to your house," he told her, and he humbly added: "I have listened to your voice." —1 Sam. 25:32-35.

"Here Is Your Slave Girl"

20 After she took her leave, Abigail could not help thinking

17, 18. How did Abigail approach David, what did she say, and what made her words effective?

19. How did David respond to Abigail's words, and why did he praise her?

20, 21. (a) What do you find admirable about Abigail's willingness to return to her husband? (b) How did Abigail show courage and discretion in choosing the time to talk to Nabal?

"Please, let your slave girl speak in your ears"

about that meeting; nor could she have failed to notice the contrast between that faithful, kind man and the brute to whom she was married. But she did not dwell on such thoughts. We read: "Later Abigail came in to Nabal." Yes, she returned to her husband as determined as ever to carry out her role as his wife to the best of her ability. She had to tell him of the gift she had given to David and his men. He had a right to know. She also had to tell him—before he learned of it elsewhere, to his even greater shame—about the danger that had been averted. She could not tell him now though. He was feasting like a king and was as drunk as could be.—1 Sam. 25:36.

²¹ Again showing both courage and discretion, she waited until the next morning when the influence of the wine had ebbed. He would be sober enough to understand her, yet possibly more dangerous in his temper as well. Still, she approached and told him the whole story. No doubt she expected him to explode in fury, perhaps violence. Instead, he just sat there, not moving. —1 Sam. 25:37.

²² What was wrong with the man? "His heart came to be dead inside him, and he himself became as a stone." Perhaps he had suffered some form of stroke. However, about ten days later, his end came—and not strictly for medical reasons. The account tells us: "Jehovah struck Nabal, so that he died." (1 Sam. 25:38) With that righteous execution, Abigail's long nightmare of a marriage was over. While Jehovah does not step in with miraculous executions today, this account is a fitting reminder that no case of domestic tyranny or abuse escapes his notice. In his own time, he will always bring about justice. **—Read Luke 8:17.**

²³ Besides the release from a bad marriage, Abigail had another blessing in store. When he learned of the death of Nabal, David sent messengers to propose marriage. "Here is your slave girl," she responded, "as a maidservant to wash the feet of the servants of my lord." Clearly, she was not changed by the prospect of

TO THINK ABOUT . . .

- What can we learn from Abigail's difficult marital situation?

- How did Abigail show courage and discretion in dealing with her husband's insult of David?

- How did Abigail speak sensibly and persuasively to David?

- In what ways would you like to imitate the faith of Abigail?

22. What happened to Nabal, and what can we learn about all cases of domestic tyranny or abuse?

23. What further blessing came to Abigail, and how did she show that her new prospects did not change her?

Abigail
courageously
told Nabal
what she had
done to save
his life

becoming David's wife; she even offered to be a servant to his servants! Then we read again of her hastening, this time to ready herself to go to David.—1 Sam. 25:39-42.

²⁴ This was no fairy-tale ending; Abigail's life with David would not always be easy. David was already married to Ahinoam, and though God permitted polygamy, it surely presented special challenges to faithful women back then. And David was not yet king; there would be obstacles and hardships to surmount before he served Jehovah in that way. But as Abigail helped and support-ed David along life's road, eventually bearing him a son, she learned that she had a husband who valued her and protected her. On one occasion he even rescued her from kidnappers! (1 Sam. 30:1-19) David thus imitated Jehovah God, who loves and values such discreet, courageous, and faithful women.

---

24. Abigail faced what challenges in her new life, but how did her husband and her God view her?

83

CHAPTER TEN

He Stood Up for Pure Worship

ELIJAH looked out over the crowd as they trudged up the slopes of Mount Carmel. Even in the dim light of early morning, the poverty and want afflicting these people were plain to see. The drought, three and a half years long, had left its mark on them.

² Among them strutted the 450 prophets of Baal, full of pride and burning hatred for Elijah, Jehovah's prophet. Queen Jezebel had executed many servants of Jehovah, but this man still stood firm against Baal worship. Ah, but for how long? Perhaps those priests reasoned that a lone man could never prevail against all of them. (1 Ki. 18:4, 19, 20) King Ahab had also come, riding in his royal chariot. He too bore no love for Elijah.

³ Ahead of that solitary prophet lay a day like no other in his life. As Elijah watched, the stage was being set for one of the most dramatic confrontations between good and evil that the world has ever seen. How did he feel as that day dawned? He was not impervious to fear, being "a man with feelings like ours." (**Read James 5:17.**) We can be sure, at least, of this much: Surrounded by the faithless people, their apostate king, and those murderous priests, Elijah keenly felt that he was all alone.—1 Ki. 18:22.

⁴ What, though, had brought Israel to this crisis? And what does this account have to do with you? Consider Elijah's example of faith and how practical it can be for us today.

A Long Struggle Reaches a Climax

⁵ For much of his life, Elijah had helplessly watched as the best thing about his homeland and his people was pushed aside

---

1, 2. (a) In what way were Elijah's people afflicted? (b) Elijah faced what opposition on Mount Carmel?

3, 4. (a) Why might Elijah have felt some fear as an important day dawned? (b) What questions will we consider?

5, 6. (a) Israel was in the grip of what struggle? (b) How had King Ahab deeply offended Jehovah?

and trampled underfoot. You see, Israel was in the grip of a long struggle, a war between pure religion and false, between the worship of Jehovah God and the idolatry of the surrounding nations. In Elijah's day, that struggle had taken an especially ugly turn.

⁶ King Ahab had deeply offended Jehovah. He married Jezebel, the daughter of the king of Sidon. Jezebel was determined to spread Baal worship in the land of Israel and to eradicate the worship of Jehovah. Ahab quickly fell under her influence. He built a temple and an altar to Baal and took the lead in bowing down to this pagan god.—1 Ki. 16:30-33.

⁷ What made Baal worship so offensive? It seduced Israel, luring many away from the true God. It was also a disgusting and brutal religion. It involved male and female temple prostitution, sexual orgies, and even the sacrifice of children. Jehovah responded by sending Elijah to Ahab to announce a drought that would last until God's prophet proclaimed its end. (1 Ki. 17:1) Several years passed before Elijah showed himself to Ahab and told him to gather the people and the Baal prophets to Mount Carmel.*

> In a sense, the most potent elements that characterized Baal worship are thriving today

⁸ What, though, does this struggle mean for us today? Some might assume that a story about Baal worship is irrelevant now, since we do not see temples and altars to Baal around us. But this account is not mere ancient history. (Rom. 15:4) The word "Baal" means "owner" or "master." Jehovah told his people that they should choose him as their "baal," or husbandly owner. (Isa. 54:5) Would you not agree that people still serve a variety of masters other than God Almighty? Whether people use their life in the service of money, career, recreation, sexual pleasure, or any of the countless gods that are worshipped instead of Jehovah, they choose a master. (Matt. 6:24; *read Romans 6:16.*) In a sense, the most potent elements that characterized Baal worship

---

* See the box "How Long Was the Drought in Elijah's Day?"

---

7. (a) What made Baal worship so offensive? (b) Regarding the length of the drought in Elijah's day, why may we be sure that the Bible contains no contradiction? (Include the box.)

8. What does this account about Baal worship mean for us today?

are thriving today. Reflecting on that ancient contest between Jehovah and Baal can help us make a wise choice about whom we will serve.

"Limping"—How?

9 The heights of Mount Carmel commanded a sweeping view —from the torrent valley of Kishon below to the Great Sea (Mediterranean Sea) nearby and to the mountains of Lebanon on the far northern horizon.* But as the sun rose on this climactic day, the vista was grim. A deathly pall hung over the once fertile land that Jehovah had given to the children of Abraham. It was now

---

* Mount Carmel is usually lush and green, as moisture-laden winds from the sea rise along its slopes, frequently depositing rains and plentiful dew. Because Baal was credited with bringing rain, this mount was evidently an important site for Baal worship. A barren, dry Carmel thus made an ideal spot to expose Baalism as a fraud.

---

9. (a) How did the setting make Mount Carmel an ideal spot to expose Baalism? (See also footnote.) (b) What did Elijah say to the people?

How Long Was the Drought in Elijah's Day?

Jehovah's prophet Elijah announced to King Ahab that the long drought would end soon. That happened "in the third year" —evidently counting from the day Elijah first announced the drought. (1 Ki. 18:1) Jehovah sent rain soon after Elijah said that He would. Some might conclude that the drought ended during the course of its third year and that it was therefore less than three years long. However, both Jesus and James tell us that the drought lasted "three years and six months." (Luke 4:25; Jas. 5:17) Is this a contradiction?

Not at all. You see, the dry season in ancient Israel was quite long, lasting up to six months. No doubt Elijah came to Ahab to announce the drought when the dry season was already proving to be unusually long and severe. In effect, the drought had begun nearly half a year earlier. Thus, when Elijah announced the end of the drought "in the third year" from his previous announcement, the drought had already lasted nearly three and a half years. The full "three years and six months" had elapsed by the time all the people assembled to witness the great test on Mount Carmel.

Consider, then, the timing of Elijah's first visit to Ahab. The people believed that Baal was "the rider of the clouds," the god who would bring rains to end the dry season. If the dry season was unusually long, people likely wondered: 'Where is Baal? When will he bring the rains?' Elijah's announcement that neither rain nor dew would occur until he said so must have been devastating to those Baal worshippers.—1 Ki. 17:1.

a land baked hard by the merciless sun, ruined by the folly of God's own people! As those people thronged, Elijah approached them and spoke: "How long will you be limping upon two different opinions? If Jehovah is the true God, go following him; but if Baal is, go following him."—1 Ki. 18:21.

¹⁰ What did Elijah mean by the expression "limping upon two different opinions"? Well, those people did not realize that they had to choose between the worship of Jehovah and the worship of Baal. They thought that they could have it both ways —that they could appease Baal with their revolting rituals and still ask favors of Jehovah God. Perhaps they reasoned that Baal would bless their crops and herds, while "Jehovah of armies" would protect them in battle. (1 Sam. 17:45) They had forgotten a basic truth—one that still eludes many today. Jehovah does not share his worship with anyone. He demands and is worthy of exclusive devotion. Any worship of him that is mixed with some other form of worship is unacceptable to him, even offensive!—*Read Exodus 20:5.*

¹¹ So those Israelites were "limping" along like a man trying to follow two pathways at once. Many people today make a similar mistake, allowing other "baals" to creep into their life and push aside the worship of God. Heeding Elijah's clarion call to stop limping can help us to reexamine our own priorities and worship.

A Climactic Test

¹² Elijah next proposed a test. It was simplicity itself. The Baal priests were to set up an altar and lay out a sacrifice on it; then they were to pray to their god to light the fire. Elijah would do the same. He said that the "God that answers by fire is the true God." Elijah well knew who was the true God. So strong was his faith that he did not hesitate to give his opponents every advantage. He let those Baal prophets go first. So they chose their bull for sacrifice and approached Baal.*—1 Ki. 18:24, 25.

---

* Notably, Elijah told them: "You must not put fire to" the sacrifice. Some scholars say that such idolaters sometimes used altars with a secret cavity beneath so that a fire could appear to be lit supernaturally.

---

10. How were Elijah's people "limping upon two different opinions," and what basic truth had they forgotten?

11. How do you think that Elijah's speech on Mount Carmel can help us to reexamine our priorities and worship?

12, 13. (a) What test did Elijah propose? (b) How might we show that we are just as confident as Elijah was?

13 We do not live in an age of miracles. However, Jehovah has not changed. We can be just as confident in him as Elijah was. For instance, when others disagree with what the Bible teaches, we need not fear to let them go ahead and have their say. Like Elijah, we can look to the true God to settle the matter. We do that by relying, not on ourselves, but on his inspired Word, which is designed "for setting things straight."—2 Tim. 3:16.

14 The Baal prophets proceeded to set up their sacrifice and call on their god. "O Baal, answer us!" they cried again and again. They kept at it as the minutes and then the hours passed by. "But there was no voice, and there was no one answering," the Bible says. At noon Elijah began to mock them, asserting sarcastically that Baal must be too busy to answer them, that he was relieving himself in the privy, or that he was napping and someone needed to wake him up. "Call at the top of your voice," Elijah urged those charlatans. Clearly, he saw this Baal worship as ridiculous fakery, and he wanted God's people to see it for the fraud that it was.—1 Ki. 18:26, 27.

> Elijah saw Baal worship as ridiculous fakery, and he wanted God's people to see it for the fraud that it was

15 In response, the Baal priests became even more frenzied, "calling at the top of their voice and cutting themselves according to their custom with daggers and with lances, until they caused blood to flow out upon them." All to no avail! "There was no voice, and there was no one answering, and there was no paying of attention." (1 Ki. 18: 28, 29) Indeed, there was no Baal. He was an invention designed by Satan to lure people away from Jehovah. The truth is, choosing any master other than Jehovah leads to disappointment, even shame.—*Read Psalm 25:3; 115:4-8.*

The Answer

16 Late in the afternoon came Elijah's turn to offer a sacrifice. He repaired an altar to Jehovah that had been torn down,

---

14. In what way did Elijah mock the Baal prophets, and why?

15. How does the case of the Baal priests show the folly of choosing any master other than Jehovah?

16. (a) Elijah's repair of the altar to Jehovah on Mount Carmel may have reminded the people of what? (b) How did Elijah further show his confidence in his God?

"At that the fire of Jehovah came falling"

no doubt by enemies of pure worship. He used 12 stones, perhaps reminding many in the 10-tribe nation of Israel that the Law given to all 12 tribes was still binding on them. Then he laid out his sacrifice and had everything doused with water, possibly obtained from the Mediterranean Sea nearby. He even had a trench dug around the altar and filled it with water. Just as he had given the prophets of Baal every advantage, he gave Jehovah every disadvantage—such was his confidence in his God.—1 Ki. 18:30-35.

> Elijah's prayer showed that he still cared about his people, for he was eager to see Jehovah turn "their heart back"

¹⁷ When everything was ready, Elijah said a prayer. Eloquent in its simplicity, the prayer showed clearly where Elijah's priorities lay. First and foremost, he wanted it known that Jehovah, not this Baal, was "God in Israel." Second, he wanted everyone to know that his own role was that of Jehovah's servant; all glory and credit should go to God. Finally, he showed that he still cared about his people, for he was eager to see Jehovah turn "their heart back." (1 Ki. 18:36, 37) Despite all the misery that they had caused by their faithlessness, Elijah still loved them. In our own prayers to God, can we manifest similar humility, concern for God's name, and compassion for others who need help?

¹⁸ Before Elijah's prayer, the crowds there might have wondered if Jehovah would turn out to be an empty lie, as Baal had proved to be. After the prayer, though, there was no time for wondering. The account says: "At that the fire of Jehovah came falling and went eating up the burnt offering and the pieces of wood and the stones and the dust, and the water that was in the trench it licked up." (1 Ki. 18:38) What a spectacular answer! And how did the people respond?

¹⁹ "Jehovah is the true God! Jehovah is the true God!" they cried out, all of them. (1 Ki. 18:39) At last they saw the truth. However, they had not as yet shown any faith. Frankly, to admit that Jehovah is the true God after seeing fire fall from heav-

---

17. How did Elijah's prayer reveal his priorities, and how can we imitate his example in our own prayers?

18, 19. (a) How did Jehovah answer Elijah's prayer? (b) What did Elijah order the people to do, and why did the Baal priests deserve no mercy?

en in response to a prayer is not an impressive demonstration of faith. So Elijah asked more of them. He asked them to do what they should have done many years earlier—obey the Law of Jehovah. God's Law said that false prophets and idolaters should be put to death. (Deut. 13:5-9) These Baal priests were committed enemies of Jehovah God, and they deliberately worked against his purposes. Did they deserve mercy? Well, what mercy had they ever granted to all those innocent children who were burned alive as sacrifices to Baal? (**Read Proverbs 21:13;** Jer. 19:5) Those men were well beyond the reach of mercy! So Elijah ordered that they be executed, and executed they were.—1 Ki. 18:40.

20 Modern-day critics may decry the conclusion to this test on Mount Carmel. Some people may worry lest religious zealots use it to justify violent acts of religious intolerance. And sadly, there are many violent religious fanatics today. However, Elijah was no fanatic. He was acting on Jehovah's behalf in a just execution. Furthermore, genuine Christians know that they cannot follow Elijah's course in taking a sword to the wicked. Rather, they follow the standard for all disciples of Jesus as found in Christ's words to Peter: "Return your sword to its place, for all those who take the sword will perish by the sword." (Matt. 26:52) Jehovah will use his Son to carry out divine justice in the future.

21 The responsibility of a true Christian is to lead a life of faith. (John 3:16) One way to do so is to imitate faithful men like Elijah. He worshipped Jehovah exclusively and urged others to do the same. He boldly exposed as fraudulent a religion that Satan used to lure people away from Jehovah. And he trusted Jehovah to settle matters instead of relying on his own abilities and will. Elijah stood up for pure worship. May all of us imitate his faith!

TO THINK ABOUT . . .

- What can we learn from Elijah about worshipping Jehovah exclusively?

- How can we imitate Elijah when dealing with those who disagree with what the Bible teaches?

- What can we learn from Elijah's prayer on Mount Carmel?

- In what ways would you like to imitate the faith of Elijah?

---

20. Why are the concerns of modern-day critics about Elijah's execution of the Baal priests unfounded?

21. How is Elijah's example a fitting one for true Christians today?

CHAPTER ELEVEN

He Watched, and He Waited

ELIJAH longed to be alone with his heavenly Father. But the throngs around him had just seen this true prophet call down fire from heaven, and many of the people were no doubt eager to curry favor with him. Before Elijah could ascend to the heights of Mount Carmel and approach Jehovah God in private prayer, he faced an unpleasant task. He had to speak to King Ahab.

² The two men could hardly have been more different. Ahab, bedecked in royal finery, was a greedy, weak-willed apostate. Elijah wore the official garb of a prophet—a simple, rustic robe, possibly of animal skin or of woven camel or goat hair. He was a man of great courage, integrity, and faith. The day that was now drawing to a close had revealed much about the character of each man.

³ It had been a bad day for Ahab and other Baal worshippers. The pagan religion that Ahab and his wife, Queen Jezebel, championed in the ten-tribe kingdom of Israel had been dealt a severe blow. Baal had been exposed as a fraud. That lifeless god had failed to light a simple fire in response to the frantic pleas, dances, and ritual bloodletting of his prophets. Baal had failed to protect those 450 men from their well-deserved execution. But the false god had failed in something else, and that failure was about to be made complete. For over three years, the Baal prophets had implored their god to end the drought afflicting the land, but Baal had proved unable to do so. Soon, Jehovah himself would demonstrate his supremacy by ending the drought.—1 Ki. 16:30–17:1; 18:1-40.

⁴ When, though, would Jehovah act? How would Elijah con-

1, 2. Elijah faced what unpleasant task, and in what ways were he and Ahab different?

3, 4. (a) Why had it been a bad day for Ahab and other Baal worshippers? (b) What questions will we discuss?

duct himself until then? And what can we learn from this man of faith? Let us see as we examine the account.—*Read 1 Kings 18:41-46.*

A Prayerful Attitude

⁵ Elijah approached Ahab and said: "Go up, eat and drink; for there is the sound of the turmoil of a downpour." Had this wicked king learned anything from the day's events? The account does not say specifically, but we find here no words of repentance, no request that the prophet help him approach Jehovah and seek forgiveness. No, Ahab simply "proceeded to go up to eat and drink." (1 Ki. 18:41, 42) What about Elijah?

⁶ "As for Elijah, he went up to the top of Carmel and began crouching to the earth and keeping his face put between his knees." While Ahab went off to fill his stomach, Elijah had an opportunity to pray to his heavenly Father. Note the humble posture described here—Elijah on the ground with his head

---

5. What did Elijah tell Ahab to do, and does it seem that Ahab had learned anything from the day's events?

6, 7. For what did Elijah pray, and why?

Elijah's prayers reflected his earnest desire to see God's will done

bowed so low that his face was near his knees. What was Elijah doing? We need not guess. The Bible, at James 5:18, tells us that Elijah prayed for the drought to end. Likely he was offering such a prayer on top of Carmel.

⁷ Earlier, Jehovah had said: "I am determined to give rain upon the surface of the ground." (1 Ki. 18:1) So Elijah prayed for the fulfillment of Jehovah's stated will, much as Jesus taught his followers to pray some one thousand years later.—Matt. 6: 9, 10.

Elijah eagerly sought evidence that Jehovah was about to act

⁸ Elijah's example teaches us much about prayer. Foremost in Elijah's thoughts was the accomplishment of God's will. When we pray, it is good to remember: "No matter what it is that we ask according to [God's] will, he hears us." (1 John 5:14) Clearly, then, we need to know what God's will is in order to pray acceptably—a good reason to make Bible study a part of our daily life. Surely Elijah also wanted to see an end to the drought because of all the suffering among the people of his homeland. His heart was likely full of thanksgiving after the miracle he had seen Jehovah perform that day. We likewise want our prayers to reflect heartfelt thanksgiving and concern for the welfare of others.—*Read 2 Corinthians 1:11; Philippians 4:6.*

Confident and Watchful

⁹ Elijah was sure that Jehovah would act to end the drought, but he was not sure *when* Jehovah would act. So, what did the prophet do in the meantime? Note what the account says: "He said to his attendant: 'Go up, please. Look in the direction of the sea.' So he went up and looked and then said: 'There is nothing at all.' And he went on to say, 'Go back,' for seven times." (1 Ki. 18:43) Elijah's example teaches us at least two lessons. First, note the prophet's confidence. Then, consider his watchfulness.

¹⁰ Because Elijah had confidence in Jehovah's promise, he eagerly sought evidence that Jehovah was about to act. He sent

8. What does Elijah's example teach us about prayer?

9. What did Elijah direct his attendant to do, and what two qualities will we consider?

10, 11. (a) In what way did Elijah show his confidence in Jehovah's promise? (b) Why can we have similar confidence?

his attendant up to a high vantage point to scan the horizon for any signs of impending rain. Upon his return, the attendant delivered this unenthusiastic report: "There is nothing at all." The horizon was clear, and the sky, evidently cloudless. Now, did you notice something unusual? Remember, Elijah had just told King Ahab: "There is the sound of the turmoil of a downpour." How could the prophet say such a thing when there were no rain clouds to be seen?

[11] Elijah knew of Jehovah's promise. As Jehovah's prophet and representative, he was sure that his God would fulfill His word. Elijah was confident—so much so that it was as if he could already hear the downpour. We might be reminded of the Bible's description of Moses: "He continued steadfast as seeing the One who is invisible." Is God that real to you? He provides ample reason for us to put that kind of faith in him and his promises.—Heb. 11:1, 27.

[12] Next, notice how watchful Elijah was. He sent his attendant back, not once or twice, but seven times! We might imagine the attendant tiring of such a repetitive task, but Elijah remained eager for a sign and did not give up. Finally, after his seventh trip, the attendant reported: "Look! There is a small cloud like a man's palm ascending out of the sea." Can you picture that attendant holding his arm outstretched and using his palm to gauge the size of one little cloud coming up over the horizon of the Great Sea? The attendant may have been unimpressed. To Elijah, though, that cloud was significant. He now gave his attendant urgent directions: "Go up, say to Ahab, 'Hitch up! And go down that the downpour may not detain you!'" —1 Ki. 18:44.

[13] Again, Elijah set a powerful example for us. We too live at a time when God will soon act to fulfill his stated purpose. Elijah awaited the end of a drought; God's servants today await the end of a corrupt world system of things. (1 John 2:17) Until Jehovah God acts, we must keep ever on the watch, as Elijah did. God's own Son, Jesus, advised his followers: "Keep on the watch, therefore, because you do not know on what day your Lord is coming." (Matt. 24:42) Did Jesus mean that his followers would be completely in the dark as to when the end would

---

12. How did Elijah show that he was watchful, and how did he react to the news that there was one little cloud?

13, 14. (a) How can we imitate Elijah's watchfulness? (b) What reasons do we have for acting with urgency?

"A great downpour began to occur"

come? No, for he spoke at length about what the world would be like in the days leading up to the end. All of us can observe the fulfillment of this detailed sign of "the conclusion of the system of things."—*Read Matthew 24:3-7.*

14 Each facet of that sign furnishes powerful, convincing evidence. Is such evidence enough to move us to act with urgency in our service to Jehovah? One little cloud rising from the horizon was enough to convince Elijah that Jehovah was about to act. Was the faithful prophet disappointed?

Jehovah Brings Relief and Blessings

15 The account tells us: "It came about in the meantime that the heavens themselves darkened up with clouds and wind and a great downpour began to occur. And Ahab kept riding and made his way to Jezreel." (1 Ki. 18:45) Events began to unfold at remarkable speed. While Elijah's attendant was delivering the prophet's message to Ahab, that little cloud became many, filling and darkening the sky. A great wind blew. At last, after three and a half years, rain fell on the soil of Israel. The parched ground drank in the drops. As the rain became a downpour, the river Kishon swelled, no doubt washing away the blood of the executed Baal prophets. The wayward Israelites too were being given a chance to wash away the terrible stain of Baal worship on the land.

One little cloud was enough to convince Elijah that Jehovah was about to act. The sign of the last days gives compelling reasons to act with urgency

16 Surely Elijah hoped that it would be so! Perhaps he wondered how Ahab would respond to the dramatic events that were unfolding. Would Ahab repent and turn away from the pollution of Baal worship? The events of the day had furnished powerful reasons to make such changes. Of course, we cannot know what was going through Ahab's mind at the moment. The account simply tells us that the king "kept riding and made his way to Jezreel." Had he learned anything? Was he resolved to change his ways? Later events suggest that the answer is no. Still, the day was not yet over for Ahab—nor for Elijah.

15, 16. What events unfolded rapidly, and what might Elijah have wondered about Ahab?

97

17 Jehovah's prophet began to make his way along the same road Ahab had taken. A long, dark, wet trek lay ahead of him. But something unusual happened next.

18 "The very hand of Jehovah proved to be upon Elijah, so that he girded up his hips and went running ahead of Ahab all the way to Jezreel." (1 Ki. 18:46) Clearly, "the very hand of Jehovah" was acting on Elijah in a supernatural way. Jezreel was 19 miles distant, and Elijah was no youth.* Just picture that prophet girding up his long garments, tying them at his hips so that his legs would have freedom of movement, and then running along that rain-drenched road—running so fast that he caught up with, passed, and outpaced the royal chariot!

19 What a blessing that must have been for Elijah! To feel such strength, vitality, and stamina—perhaps even more than he had ever felt in his youth—must have proved a thrilling experience. We might recall the prophecies that guarantee perfect health and vigor to faithful ones in the coming earthly Paradise. (*Read Isaiah 35:6;* Luke 23:43) As Elijah raced along that wet road, he surely knew that he had the approval of his Father, the only true God, Jehovah!

20 Jehovah is eager to bless us. Let us reach out for his blessings; they are worth every effort we can make. Like Elijah, we need to be watchful, carefully weighing the powerful evidence showing that Jehovah is about to act in these dangerous and urgent times. Like Elijah, we have every reason to place complete confidence in the promises of Jehovah, "the God of truth."—Ps. 31:5.

TO THINK ABOUT . . .

- How did Elijah show a prayerful attitude?

- How did Elijah display his confidence in Jehovah's promise?

- Elijah set what example regarding watchfulness?

- What would you like to do in order to imitate Elijah's faith?

---

* Soon after this, Jehovah would assign Elijah to train Elisha, who would become known as the one "who poured out water upon the hands of Elijah." (2 Ki. 3:11) Elisha acted as Elijah's attendant, evidently offering practical assistance to an older man.

17, 18. (a) What happened to Elijah on the road to Jezreel? (b) What was remarkable about Elijah's running from Carmel to Jezreel? (See also footnote.)

19. (a) Elijah's God-given energy and stamina may remind us of what prophecies? (b) As Elijah ran to Jezreel, what did he surely know?

20. How can we reach out for Jehovah's blessings?

CHAPTER TWELVE

He Took Comfort in His God

ELIJAH ran through the rain as the darkness deepened. He had a long way to go before he would reach Jezreel, and he was no young man. Yet, he ran on tirelessly, for "the very hand of Jehovah" was upon him. The energy coursing through his body was surely unlike any he had ever known. Why, he had just outpaced the team of horses that was pulling King Ahab in his royal chariot!—*Read 1 Kings 18:46.*

² Now the open road lay before him. Imagine Elijah blinking the raindrops from his eyes as he ran, thinking back over the most eventful day of his life. Without question, it was a glorious victory for Elijah's God, Jehovah, and for true worship. Far behind him, lost in the gloom of the storm, lay the windswept heights of Mount Carmel, where Jehovah had used Elijah to strike a mighty and miraculous blow against Baal worship. Hundreds of Baal prophets were exposed as wicked frauds and justly executed. Then Elijah prayed to Jehovah for an end to the drought that had afflicted the land for three and a half years. The rains fell!—1 Ki. 18:18-45.

³ As Elijah splashed along those 19 miles to Jezreel, his hopes might have been high. It may have seemed to him that a real turning point had come at last. Ahab would have to change! After what he had witnessed, surely he had no choice but to abandon Baal worship; to restrain his queen, Jezebel; and to stop the persecution of Jehovah's servants.

⁴ When things seem to be going our way, it is only natural that our hopes rise. We may imagine that our lot in life will continue to improve, perhaps even thinking that our worst problems are finally behind us. If Elijah thought that way, no wonder,

1, 2. What happened on the most eventful day of Elijah's life?

3, 4. (a) Why might Elijah's hopes have been high as he made his way to Jezreel? (b) What questions will we consider?

"Elijah . . . went running ahead of Ahab all the way to Jezreel"

for he "was a man with feelings like ours." (Jas. 5:17) Actually, though, Elijah's problems were far from over. In fact, within hours Elijah would be so fearful, so low in spirits, that he would wish to die. What happened, and how did Jehovah help his prophet to renew his faith and his courage? Let us see.

An Unexpected Turn of Events

5 When Ahab reached his palace in Jezreel, did he give any evidence of being a changed man? We read: "Ahab told Jezebel all that Elijah had done and all about how he had killed all the prophets with the sword." (1 Ki. 19:1) Notice that Ahab's account of the day's events left out Elijah's God, Jehovah. A fleshly man, Ahab saw the day's miraculous events in strictly human terms —what "Elijah had done." Clearly, he had not learned to respect Jehovah God. And how did his vengeful wife react?

6 Jezebel was furious! Livid with rage, she sent this message to Elijah: "So may the gods do, and so may they add to it, if at this time tomorrow I shall not make your soul like the soul of each one of them!" (1 Ki. 19:2) This was a death threat of the worst kind. In effect, Jezebel was vowing that she herself should die if she could not have Elijah killed within the day to avenge her Baal prophets. Imagine Elijah being awakened from sleep in some humble lodging in Jezreel on that stormy night—only to hear the queen's messenger deliver those awful words. How was he affected?

Overcome by Discouragement and Fear

7 If Elijah cherished any notions that the war against Baal worship was all but over, his hopes came crashing down at that moment. Jezebel was undeterred. A great many of Elijah's faithful colleagues had already been executed on her orders, and now, it seemed, he was to be next. What effect did Jezebel's threat have on Elijah? The Bible tells us: "He became afraid." Did Elijah picture in his mind's eye the terrible death that Jezebel had in store for him? If he dwelled on such thoughts, it is no wonder that his courage failed him. At any rate, Elijah "began to go for his soul" —he ran for his life.—1 Ki. 18:4; 19:3.

---

5. After the events on Mount Carmel, had Ahab learned to respect Jehovah more, and how do we know?

6. What message did Jezebel send to Elijah, and what did it mean?

7. What effect did Jezebel's threat have on Elijah, and what did he do?

⁸ Elijah was not the only man of faith ever to be overcome by fear. Much later, the apostle Peter had a similar problem. For instance, when Jesus enabled Peter to join Him in walking on water, the apostle began "looking at the windstorm." He then lost his courage and started to sink. (**Read Matthew 14:30.**) The examples of Elijah and Peter thus teach us a valuable lesson. If we want to maintain our courage, we must not let our mind dwell on the dangers that frighten us. We need to keep our focus on the Source of our hope and strength.

"It Is Enough!"

⁹ Driven by fear, Elijah fled southwestward some 95 miles to Beer-sheba, a town near the southern border of Judah. There he left his attendant behind and struck out into the wilderness alone. The record says that he went "a day's journey," so we may picture him starting off at sunrise, evidently carrying no provisions with him. Depressed, spurred ever onward by fear, he struggled over the rough and wild terrain under the blazing sun. As that glaring disk gradually reddened and sank to the horizon, Elijah's strength gave out. Exhausted, he sat down under a broom tree —the closest thing to shelter in that barren landscape.—1 Ki. 19:4.

¹⁰ Elijah prayed in utter desperation. He asked to die. He said: "I am no better than my forefathers." He knew that his forefathers were then mere dust and bones in the grave, unable to do any good for anybody. (Eccl. 9:10) Elijah felt just as worthless. No wonder he cried out: "It is enough!" Why go on living?

¹¹ Should it be shocking to learn that a man of God could become so low in spirits? Not necessarily. A number of faithful men and women in the Bible record are described as feeling so sad that they wished for death—among them Rebekah, Jacob, Moses, and Job.—Gen. 25:22; 37:35; Num. 11:13-15; Job 14:13.

> If we want to maintain our courage, we must not let our mind dwell on the dangers that frighten us

8. (a) How was Peter's problem similar to that of Elijah? (b) What lesson can we learn from Elijah and Peter?

9. Describe Elijah's journey and his state of mind as he fled.

10, 11. (a) What was the meaning of Elijah's prayer to Jehovah? (b) Using the cited scriptures, describe the feelings of other godly individuals who became low in spirits.

12 Today, we live in "critical times hard to deal with," so it is not surprising that many people, even faithful servants of God, find themselves feeling low at times. (2 Tim. 3:1) If you ever find yourself in such a dire situation, follow Elijah's example in this respect: Pour out your feelings to God. After all, Jehovah is "the God of all comfort." (**Read 2 Corinthians 1:3, 4.**) Did he comfort Elijah?

Jehovah Sustained His Prophet

13 How do you think Jehovah felt as he looked down from heaven and saw his beloved prophet lying under that tree in the wilderness and begging for death to take him? We do not have to guess. After Elijah sank into sleep, Jehovah sent an angel to him. The angel gently woke Elijah with a touch and said: "Rise up, eat." Elijah did so, for the angel had kindly set out a simple meal for him—fresh, warm bread along with water. Did he even thank the angel? The record says only that the prophet ate and drank and went back to sleep. Was he too despondent to speak? At any rate, the angel woke him a second time, perhaps at dawn. Once more, he urged Elijah, "Rise up, eat," and he added these remarkable words, "for the journey is too much for you."—1 Ki. 19:5-7.

14 Thanks to God-given insight, the angel knew where Elijah was headed. He also knew that the journey would be too much for Elijah to carry out in his own strength. What a comfort to serve a God who knows our goals and our limitations better than we do! (**Read Psalm 103:13, 14.**) How did Elijah benefit from that meal?

15 We read: "He rose up and ate and drank, and he kept going in the power of that nourishment for forty days and forty nights as far as the mountain of the true God, Horeb." (1 Ki. 19:8) Like Moses some six centuries before him and Jesus nearly ten centuries after him, Elijah fasted for 40 days and 40 nights. (Ex. 34:28; Luke 4:1, 2) That one meal did not make all his problems go away, but it sustained him miraculously. Imagine that

---

12. If you ever find yourself feeling very low, in what respect should you follow Elijah's example?

13, 14. (a) How did Jehovah by means of an angel show loving concern for His troubled prophet? (b) Why is it comforting that Jehovah knows all about each one of us, including our limitations?

15, 16. (a) What did nourishment from Jehovah enable Elijah to do? (b) Why should we appreciate the way that Jehovah sustains his servants today?

older man trudging through the trackless wilderness day after day, week after week, for nearly a month and a half!

¹⁶ Jehovah sustains his servants today as well, not with miraculous physical meals, but in a far more vital way. He provides for his servants spiritually. (Matt. 4:4) Learning about God from his Word and from publications that are carefully based on the Bible sustains us spiritually. Taking in such spiritual nourishment may not make all our problems go away, but it can help us endure what might otherwise be unendurable. It also leads to "everlasting life."—John 17:3.

¹⁷ Elijah walked nearly 200 miles until he finally reached Mount Horeb. It was a place of great significance, for there Jehovah God through an angel had long before appeared to Moses in the burning thornbush and there Jehovah had later made the Law covenant with Israel. Elijah found shelter in a cave.

How Jehovah Comforted and Strengthened His Prophet

¹⁸ At Horeb, Jehovah's "word"—evidently delivered by a spirit messenger—posed this simple question: "What is your business here, Elijah?" The question was likely spoken in a gentle way, for Elijah took it as an invitation to pour out his feelings. And pour them out he did! He said: "I have been absolutely jealous for Jehovah the God of armies; for the sons of Israel have left your covenant, your altars they have torn down, and your prophets they have killed with the sword, so that I only am left; and they begin looking for my soul to take it away." (1 Ki. 19:9, 10) Elijah's words reveal at least three reasons for his low spirits.

¹⁹ First, Elijah felt that his work had been in vain. Despite years of being "absolutely jealous" in serving Jehovah, putting God's sacred name and worship above all else, Elijah saw that conditions seemed only to have grown worse. The people were still faithless and rebellious, while false worship was running rampant. Second, Elijah felt alone. "I only am left," he said, as if in that nation he were the last man who still served Jehovah. Third, Elijah was scared. Many of his fellow prophets had already been killed, and he was convinced that he was next. It may not have been easy for Elijah to admit to those feelings, but he did not let pride or embarrassment hold him back. By opening his heart to his God in prayer, he set a good example for all faithful people.—Ps. 62:8.

17. Where did Elijah go, and why was that place significant?
18, 19. (a) Jehovah's spirit messenger posed what question, and how did Elijah respond? (b) Elijah revealed what three reasons for his low spirits?

Jehovah used his awesome power to comfort and encourage Elijah

20 How did Jehovah address Elijah's fears and concerns? The angel told Elijah to stand at the mouth of the cave. He obeyed, not knowing what was in store. A mighty wind sprang up! It must have emitted a deafening roar, for it was so powerful that it tore mountains and crags apart. Picture Elijah trying to shield his eyes while clinging to his heavy, rustic garment of hair as the gusts whipped it about him. Then he had to struggle to keep his footing, for the very earth began to heave and toss—an earthquake shook the region! He had barely recovered when a great fire swept through, forcing him back into the cave to shield himself from the searing heat.—1 Ki. 19:11, 12.

21 In each case, the account reminds us that Jehovah was not to be found within these spectacular displays of nature's power. Elijah knew that Jehovah was not some mythical nature god such as Baal, who was hailed by his deluded worshippers as "the rider of the clouds," or bringer of rains. Jehovah is the real Source of all the awesome power found in nature, but he is also vastly greater than anything he has made. Even the physical heavens cannot contain him! (1 Ki. 8:27) How did all of this help Elijah? Remember his fear. With a God like Jehovah on his side, a God who had all that overwhelming power at His disposal, Elijah had nothing to fear from Ahab and Jezebel!—*Read Psalm 118:6.*

The Bible can be like that "calm, low voice" if we let it guide us today

22 After the fire was gone, a hush fell and Elijah heard "a calm, low voice." It invited Elijah to express himself again, and he did so, pouring out his concerns a second time.* Perhaps that brought him further relief. Undoubtedly, though, Elijah found even more comfort in what the "calm, low voice" told him next. Jehovah reassured Elijah that he was far from worthless. How so? God revealed much

---

* The source of this "calm, low voice" may have been the same spirit who was used to deliver "Jehovah's word" mentioned at 1 Kings 19:9. In verse 15, this spirit is referred to simply as "Jehovah." We might be reminded of the spirit emissary whom Jehovah used to guide Israel in the wilderness and of whom God said: "My name is within him." (Ex. 23:21) We cannot be dogmatic on this point, of course, but it is worth noting that in his prehuman existence, Jesus served as "the Word," the special Spokesman to Jehovah's servants.—John 1:1.

20, 21. (a) Describe what Elijah witnessed from the mouth of the cave on Mount Horeb. (b) What did Jehovah's displays of power teach Elijah?
22. (a) How did the "calm, low voice" reassure Elijah that he was far from worthless? (b) Who might have been the source of the "calm, low voice"? (See footnote.)

of his long-range purpose regarding the war against Baal worship in Israel. Clearly, Elijah's work had not been in vain, for God's purpose was moving inexorably forward. Furthermore, Elijah still figured in that purpose, for Jehovah sent him back to work with some specific instructions.—1 Ki. 19:12-17.

23 What about Elijah's feelings of loneliness? Jehovah did two things about that. First, he told Elijah to anoint Elisha as the prophet who would eventually succeed him. This younger man would become Elijah's companion and helper for a number of years. How practical that comfort was! Second, Jehovah revealed this thrilling news: "I have let seven thousand remain in Israel, all the knees that have not bent down to Baal, and every mouth that has not kissed him." (1 Ki. 19:18) Elijah was far from alone. It must have warmed his heart to hear of those thousands of faithful people who refused to worship Baal. They needed Elijah to keep up his faithful service, to set an example of unshakable loyalty to Jehovah in those dark times. Elijah must have been deeply touched to hear those words through Jehovah's messenger, the "calm, low voice" of his God.

24 Like Elijah, we may be awestruck by the immense natural forces evident in creation, and rightly so. Creation vividly reflects the power of the Creator. (Rom. 1:20) Jehovah still loves to use his limitless might to help his faithful servants. (2 Chron. 16:9) However, God speaks most fully to us through the pages of his Word, the Bible. (*Read Isaiah 30:21.*) In a sense, the Bible can be like that "calm, low voice" if we let it guide us today. In its precious pages, Jehovah corrects us, encourages us, and reassures us of his love.

25 Did Elijah accept the comfort Jehovah gave him on Mount Horeb? Without a doubt! Soon he was back in action, once more the bold, faithful prophet who stood up against the wickedness of false worship. If we likewise take to heart the inspired words of God, "the comfort from the Scriptures," we will be able to imitate the faith of Elijah.—Rom. 15:4.

---

23. In what two ways did Jehovah address Elijah's feelings of loneliness?

24, 25. (a) In what sense can we listen to Jehovah's "calm, low voice" today? (b) Why can we be sure that Elijah accepted the comfort Jehovah gave him?

TO THINK ABOUT . . .

- What events led Elijah to become very low in spirits?

- What feelings contributed to Elijah's discouragement?

- In what ways did Jehovah comfort Elijah?

- How will you imitate Elijah if you ever become discouraged?

CHAPTER THIRTEEN

He Learned From His Mistakes

JONAH wished he could shut out the terrible sounds. It was not just the fierce wind, which was shrieking through the ship's rigging; nor was it just the mountainous waves, which were thundering against the sides of the vessel, making her every timber creak and groan. No, far worse to Jonah were the shouts of those mariners, the captain and his crew, as they struggled to keep the ship afloat. Jonah felt sure that those men were about to die—all because of him!

² What had put Jonah in such dire straits? He had made a serious mistake in his dealings with his God, Jehovah. What had he done? Were matters beyond repair? The answers can teach us much. For example, Jonah's story helps us to see how even those with genuine faith can go astray—and how they can make amends.

> There was far more to Jonah than his negative traits

A Prophet From Galilee

³ When people think of the man Jonah, they often seem to focus on negative traits, such as his lapses into disobedience or even his hardheadedness. But there was far more to the man than that. Remember, Jonah was selected to serve as a prophet of Jehovah God. Jehovah would not have picked him for such a weighty responsibility had he been unfaithful or unrighteous.

⁴ The Bible reveals a little about Jonah's background. (**Read 2 Kings 14:25.**) He was from Gath-hepher, just two and a half

---

1, 2. (a) What had Jonah brought on himself and the mariners on the ship? (b) How can Jonah's story help us?

3-5. (a) What do people often focus on when they think of Jonah? (b) What do we know about Jonah's background? (See also footnote.) (c) Why was Jonah's service as a prophet not easy or pleasant?

miles from Nazareth, the town where Jesus Christ would grow up some eight centuries later.* Jonah served as a prophet during the reign of King Jeroboam II of the ten-tribe kingdom of Israel. The time of Elijah was long past; his successor, Elisha, had died during the reign of Jeroboam's father. Although Jehovah had used those men to wipe out Baal worship, Israel was willfully going astray again. The land was now under the influence of a king who "continued to do what was bad in Jehovah's eyes." (2 Ki. 14:24) So Jonah's service could not have been easy or pleasant. Yet, he carried it out faithfully.

⁵ One day, though, Jonah's life took a dramatic turn. He received an assignment from Jehovah that he found to be extremely difficult. What was Jehovah asking him to do?

"Get Up, Go to Nineveh"

⁶ Jehovah told Jonah: "Get up, go to Nineveh the great city, and proclaim against her that their badness has come up before me." (Jonah 1:2) It is not hard to see why this assignment might have appeared daunting. Nineveh lay some 500 miles to the east, an overland journey that would likely take about a month on foot. However, the hardships of such a trek might have seemed the easy part of the job. At Nineveh, Jonah was to deliver Jehovah's judgment message to the Assyrians, who were notoriously violent, even savage. If Jonah had seen little response among God's own people, what could he hope to see among those pagans? How would a lone servant of Jehovah fare in vast Nineveh, which would come to be called "the city of bloodshed"?—Nah. 3:1, 7.

⁷ Such thoughts may well have occurred to Jonah. We do not know. What we do know is that he ran. Jehovah had directed him to go east; Jonah headed west, and as far west as he could go. He went down to the coast, to a port city named Joppa, where he found a ship headed to Tarshish. Some scholars say that

---

* Jonah's origin in a Galilean town is noteworthy because when referring to Jesus, the Pharisees arrogantly said: "Search and see that no prophet is to be raised up out of Galilee." (John 7:52) Many translators and researchers suggest that the Pharisees were making a sweeping generalization that no prophet had ever arisen or ever could arise out of lowly Galilee. If so, those men were ignoring history as well as prophecy.—Isa. 9:1, 2.

---

6. What assignment did Jehovah give to Jonah, and why may it have appeared daunting?

7, 8. (a) Just how determined was Jonah to get away from the assignment that Jehovah had given him? (b) Why should we not judge Jonah a coward?

Tarshish was in Spain. If so, Jonah was heading some 2,200 miles away from Nineveh. Such a voyage to the far end of the Great Sea might have taken as long as a year. Jonah was that determined to get away from the assignment Jehovah had given him!—*Read Jonah 1:3.*

8 Does this mean that we can dismiss Jonah as a coward? We should not be too quick to judge him. As we shall see, he was capable of remarkable personal courage. Like all of us, though, Jonah was an imperfect human struggling with a great many faults. (Ps. 51:5) Who of us has never grappled with fear?

9 It may occasionally seem that God asks us to do what strikes us as difficult, even impossible. We may even find it daunting to preach the good news of God's Kingdom, as Christians are required to do. (Matt. 24:14) It is all too easy for us to forget the profound truth that Jesus uttered: "All things are possible with God." (Mark 10:27) If at times we lose sight of that truth, perhaps we can understand Jonah's difficulty. What, though, were the consequences of Jonah's flight?

Jehovah Disciplines His Wayward Prophet

10 We can just imagine Jonah getting himself situated on that vessel, likely a Phoenician cargo ship. He watched as the captain and his crew bustled about to get their craft under way and out of port. As the shoreline slowly receded and disappeared, Jonah may have hoped he was escaping the danger he so dreaded. But suddenly, the weather changed.

11 Strong winds churned up the sea into a nightmarish rage, with waves that might dwarf even modern-day vessels. How long did it take for that wooden craft to seem terribly small and frail, lost in a watery wilderness of towering waves and plunging canyons? Did Jonah know, at that point, what he later wrote—that "Jehovah himself hurled forth a great wind at the sea"? It is hard to say. He saw, though, that the mariners began crying out to their various gods, and he knew that no help would come from that direction. (Lev. 19:4) His account says: "As for the ship, it was about to be wrecked." (Jonah 1:4) And how could Jonah pray to the God he was running from?

9. How might we occasionally feel about an assignment from Jehovah, and what truth do we need to remember at such times?

10, 11. (a) What may Jonah have hoped as the cargo ship left port? (b) What danger came upon the ship and the crew?

¹² Feeling powerless to help, Jonah went below the deck of the ship and found a place to lie down. There, he went fast asleep.* The captain found Jonah, woke him up, and urged him to pray to his god, as everyone else was doing. Convinced that there was something supernatural about this storm, the seamen cast lots to see which of the people on board might be the cause of their trouble. No doubt Jonah's heart sank as the lots eliminated one man after another. Soon the truth was plain. Jehovah was directing the storm, as well as the lots, toward one man —Jonah!—*Read Jonah 1:5-7.*

¹³ Jonah told the sailors everything. He was a servant of the almighty God, Jehovah. This was the God he was running from and had offended, putting them all in this terrible danger. The men were aghast; Jonah could see the terror in their eyes. They asked him what they should do to him in order to save the ship and their lives. What did he say? Jonah may have shuddered to think of himself drowning in that cold, wild sea. But how could he send all these men to such a death when he knew he could save them? So he urged them: "Lift me up and hurl me into the sea, and the sea will become still for you; because I am aware that it is on my account that this great tempest is upon you." —Jonah 1:12.

¹⁴ Hardly the words of a coward, are they? It must have warmed Jehovah's heart to see Jonah's brave, self-sacrificing spirit in that dire moment. Here we see Jonah's faith at its best. We can imitate it today by putting the welfare of others ahead of our own. (John 13:34, 35) When we see someone in need, whether physically, emotionally, or spiritually, do we give of ourselves in order to help out? How we please Jehovah when we do so!

¹⁵ Perhaps the sailors were moved too, for at first they refused to comply! Instead, they did everything they could to work their

---

* The *Septuagint* stresses the depth of Jonah's slumber by adding that he snored. However, lest we judge Jonah's sleep as a sign of indifference on his part, we might recall that sometimes an urge to sleep overcomes those who are very low in spirits. During Jesus' agonizing hours in the garden of Gethsemane, Peter, James, and John were "slumbering from grief."—Luke 22:45.

---

12. (a) Why should we not be too quick to judge Jonah for sleeping as the storm raged? (See also footnote.) (b) How did Jehovah reveal the cause of the trouble?

13. (a) What did Jonah confess to the sailors? (b) What did Jonah urge the sailors to do, and why?

14, 15. (a) How can we imitate Jonah's faith at its best? (b) How did the sailors respond to Jonah's request?

way through the storm—but to no avail. The tempest only grew worse. Finally, they saw that they had no choice. Calling out to Jonah's God, Jehovah, to show them mercy, they lifted the man up and hurled him over the side, into the sea.—Jonah 1:13-15.

Jonah Finds Mercy and Deliverance

¹⁶ Jonah plummeted into the raging waves. Perhaps he struggled, floundering a bit, and saw amid a chaos of foam and spray that the ship was swiftly moving away. But the mighty breakers crashed over him and forced him under. He sank down and down, sensing that all hope was gone.

¹⁷ Jonah later described how he felt at this time. Fleeting images crossed his mind. He thought with sadness that he would never again see the beautiful temple of Jehovah in Jerusalem. He had the sensation of descending to the very depths of the sea, near the roots of the mountains, where seaweed entangled him. This, it seemed, was to be his pit, his grave.—*Read Jonah 2:2-6.*

At Jonah's urging, the sailors lifted him up and hurled him into the sea

16, 17. Describe what happened to Jonah when he was thrown from the ship. (See also the pictures.)

¹⁸ But wait! There was something moving nearby—an immense, dark shape, a living thing. Looming close, it darted at him. A great maw opened over him, engulfed him, swallowed him down!

¹⁹ This must be the end. Yet, Jonah sensed something astounding. He was still alive! He was neither crushed, nor digested, nor even suffocated. No, the breath of life was still in him, though he was in what should rightly be his grave. Slowly, Jonah became filled with awe. Without a doubt, it was his God, Jehovah, who had "appointed a great fish to swallow Jonah."*—Jonah 1:17.

²⁰ Minutes passed, stretching into hours. There, in the deepest darkness he had ever known, Jonah composed his thoughts and prayed to Jehovah God. His prayer, recorded fully in the second chapter of Jonah, is revealing. It shows that Jonah had extensive knowledge of the Scriptures, for it often refers to the Psalms. It also shows a heartwarming quality: gratitude. Jonah concluded: "As for me, with the voice of thanksgiving I will sacrifice to you. What I have vowed, I will pay. Salvation belongs to Jehovah."—Jonah 2:9.

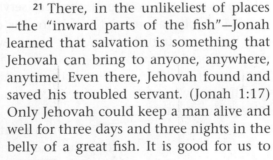

²¹ There, in the unlikeliest of places —the "inward parts of the fish"—Jonah learned that salvation is something that Jehovah can bring to anyone, anywhere, anytime. Even there, Jehovah found and saved his troubled servant. (Jonah 1:17) Only Jehovah could keep a man alive and well for three days and three nights in the belly of a great fish. It is good for us to

---

* When translated into Greek, the Hebrew word for "fish" was rendered "sea monster," or "huge fish." Although there is no way to determine exactly what kind of sea creature was involved, it has been observed that there are sharks in the Mediterranean large enough to swallow a man whole. There are far larger sharks elsewhere; the whale shark can reach up to 45 feet in length—possibly even more!

18, 19. What happened to Jonah in the depths of the sea, what kind of creature was involved, and who was behind these events? (See also footnote.)

20. What can we learn about Jonah from the prayer he uttered inside the great fish?

21. What did Jonah learn about salvation, and what valuable lesson may we remember?

remember today that Jehovah is "the God in whose hand your breath is." (Dan. 5:23) We owe our every breath, our very existence, to him. Are we grateful? Do we not, then, owe Jehovah our obedience?

²² What about Jonah? Did he learn to show his gratitude to Jehovah through obedience? He did. After three days and three nights, the fish brought Jonah right to the shore and "vomited out Jonah onto the dry land." (Jonah 2:10) Imagine—after all that, Jonah did not even have to swim ashore! Of course, he did have to find his way from that beach, wherever it was. Before long, though, his spirit of gratitude was put to the test. Jonah 3:1, 2, says: "Then the word of Jehovah occurred to Jonah the second time, saying: 'Get up, go to Nineveh the great city, and proclaim to her the proclamation that I am speaking to you.'" What would Jonah do?

²³ Jonah did not hesitate. We read: "At that, Jonah got up and went to Nineveh in accord with the word of Jehovah." (Jonah 3:3) Yes, he obeyed. Clearly, he had learned from his mistakes. In this too we need to imitate Jonah's faith. We all sin; we all make mistakes. (Rom. 3:23) But do we give up, or do we learn from our mistakes and turn to a course of obedient service to God?

²⁴ Did Jehovah reward Jonah for his obedience? Indeed he did. For one thing, it seems that Jonah eventually learned that those sailors had survived. The storm abated immediately after Jonah's self-sacrificing act, and those mariners "began to fear Jehovah greatly" and made a sacrifice to him instead of to their false gods.—Jonah 1:15, 16.

²⁵ An even greater reward came much later. Jesus used Jonah's time in the huge fish as a prophetic picture of his own time in the grave, or Sheol. (**Read Matthew 12:38-40.**) How thrilled Jonah will be to learn of that blessing when he is resurrected to life on the earth! (John 5:28, 29) Jehovah wants to bless you too. Like Jonah, will you learn from your mistakes and display an obedient, selfless spirit?

TO THINK ABOUT . . .

- Can you sympathize with Jonah's fear of an assignment from Jehovah?
- How did Jehovah show patience and mercy as he taught Jonah about obedience?
- How did Jonah show that he had learned from his mistakes?
- In what ways would you like to imitate the faith of Jonah?

22, 23. (a) How was Jonah's gratitude soon put to the test? (b) What can we learn from Jonah when it comes to the mistakes we make?

24, 25. (a) Jonah eventually received what reward in his own lifetime? (b) What rewards await Jonah in the future?

Jehovah "appointed a great fish to swallow Jonah"

CHAPTER FOURTEEN

He Learned a Lesson in Mercy

JONAH would have plenty of time to think. Before him lay a journey of more than 500 miles, an overland trek that would take him about a month, perhaps even longer. To begin, he had to choose between the shorter routes and the safer ones and then steadily make his way through valleys and over mountain passes beyond counting. He likely had to skirt the vast Syrian Desert, ford such rivers as the mighty Euphrates, and seek shelter among foreigners in the towns and villages of Syria, Mesopotamia, and Assyria. As the days passed, he thought about the destination that he so dreaded, the city that drew closer with each step he took—Nineveh.

² One thing Jonah knew for certain: He could not turn around and run away from this assignment. He had tried that before. As we saw in the preceding chapter, Jehovah patiently taught Jonah by means of a windstorm at sea and a miraculous rescue involving a huge fish. Three days later, Jonah was vomited out alive onto a beach, an awed and more compliant man.—Jonah, chaps. 1, 2.

³ When Jehovah ordered Jonah to Nineveh the second time, the prophet obediently headed east on this long journey. (**Read Jonah 3:1-3.**) However, had

---

1. What kind of journey lay ahead of Jonah, and how did he feel about his destination?

2. How had Jonah learned that he could not run away from his assignment?

3. What quality had Jehovah shown toward Jonah, yet what question arises?

he allowed Jehovah's discipline to work a thorough change in him? For instance, Jehovah had shown him mercy, saving him from drowning, holding back punishment for his rebellion, and giving him a second chance to carry out this assignment. After all of this, had Jonah learned to show mercy to others? Learning to show mercy is often difficult for imperfect humans. Let us see what we can gather from Jonah's struggle.

A Message of Judgment and a Surprising Response

4 Jonah did not see Nineveh as Jehovah did. We read: "Now Nineveh herself proved to be a city great to God." (Jonah 3:3) Three times, the record of Jonah quotes Jehovah as referring to "Nineveh the great city." (Jonah 1:2; 3:2; 4:11) Why was this city great, or important, to Jehovah?

5 Nineveh was ancient, being among the first cities that Nimrod established after the Flood. It was vast, a metropolitan region

4, 5. Why did Jehovah refer to Nineveh as "the great city," and what does that teach us about him?

Jonah found Nineveh to be a huge city full of wrongdoing

Jonah needed courage and faith to preach in Nineveh

that evidently included several other cities, requiring a man three days to walk from one end to the other. (Gen. 10:11; Jonah 3:3) Nineveh was impressive, with stately temples, mighty walls, and other edifices. But none of these factors made the city important to Jehovah God. What mattered to him were the people. Nineveh had a huge population for that time. Despite the people's badness, Jehovah cared about them. He values human life and the potential that each individual has for repenting and learning to do what is right.

6 When Jonah finally entered Nineveh, its sizable population of more than 120,000 may have made the place only more intimidating.* He walked for a day, penetrating ever deeper into that teeming metropolis, perhaps looking for a suitable central location to start spreading his message. How would he reach these people? Had he learned to speak the Assyrian tongue? Or did Jehovah grant him that ability through a miracle? We do not know. It may be that Jonah made his proclamation in his native Hebrew and used an interpreter to relate it to the Ninevites. At any rate, his message was simple and not likely to win him any favor: "Only forty days more, and Nineveh will be overthrown." (Jonah 3:4) He spoke out boldly and repeatedly. In doing so, he showed remarkable courage and faith, qualities that Christians today need more than ever.

> Jonah's message was simple and not likely to win him any favor

7 Jonah's message got the Ninevites' attention. No doubt he braced himself for a hostile and violent response. Instead, something remarkable happened. People listened! His words spread like wildfire. Before long, the whole city was talking about Jonah's prophecy of doom. (**Read Jonah 3:5.**) Rich and poor, strong and weak, young and old were all caught up in the same

---

* It has been estimated that Samaria, the capital of the ten-tribe kingdom of Israel, may have had some 20,000 to 30,000 inhabitants in Jonah's day—less than a fourth of Nineveh's population. In its heyday, Nineveh may have been the largest city in the world.

6. (a) Why might Jonah have found Nineveh intimidating? (See also footnote.) (b) What do we learn about Jonah from the preaching work that he carried out?

7, 8. (a) How did the people of Nineveh respond to Jonah's message? (b) What did the king of Nineveh do in response to Jonah's proclamation?

119

repentant spirit. They abstained from food. News of this popular movement soon reached the ears of the king.

8 The king too responded to Jonah's proclamation. Struck with godly fear, he rose up from his throne, removed his luxurious robes of state, put on the same rough clothing that his people were wearing, and even "sat down in the ashes." With his "great ones," or nobles, he issued a decree that turned the fast from a spontaneous popular movement into an official action of state. He ordered that all wear sackcloth, even the domestic animals.* He humbly acknowledged that his people were guilty of badness and violence. Expressing hope that the true God would soften upon seeing their repentance, the king said: "God may . . . turn back from his burning anger, so that we may not perish."—Jonah 3:6-9.

> God is eager to see the wicked repent and change their ways, as the Ninevites did

9 Some critics express doubt that such a change of heart could have occurred so quickly among the Ninevites. However, Bible scholars have noted that a movement of that kind was not out of keeping with the superstitious and volatile nature of people of such cultures in ancient times. Further, we know that such critics are mistaken, for Jesus Christ himself later referred to the repentance of the Ninevites. (**Read Matthew 12:41.**) Jesus knew what he was talking about, for he had been alive in heaven to witness those events as they unfolded. (John 8:57, 58) The truth is, we should never assume that it is impossible for people to repent—no matter how vicious they may seem to us. Only Jehovah can read what lies within the human heart.

A Contrast Between Divine Mercy and Human Rigidity

10 How did Jehovah react to the Ninevites' repentance? Jonah later wrote: "The true God got to see their works, that they

---

* This detail may seem odd, but it is not without precedent in ancient times. Greek historian Herodotus noted that the ancient Persians grieved over the death of a popular general by including their livestock in the customs of mourning.

---

9. Critics have expressed what doubt regarding the Ninevites, but how do we know that the critics are mistaken?

10, 11. (a) How did Jehovah respond to the repentance of the Ninevites? (b) Why can we be sure that Jehovah's judgment was not in error?

had turned back from their bad way; and so the true God felt regret over the calamity that he had spoken of causing to them; and he did not cause it."—Jonah 3:10.

¹¹ Does this mean that Jehovah decided that his own judgment about Nineveh had been in error? No. The Bible explains that Jehovah's justice is perfect. (**Read Deuteronomy 32:4.**) Jehovah's righteous anger against Nineveh simply abated. He observed the change in those people and saw that the punishment he had intended to bring on them would no longer be fitting. This was an occasion to show divine mercy.

¹² Jehovah is nothing like the rigid, cold, even harsh God so often portrayed by religious leaders. On the contrary, he is reasonable, adaptable, and merciful. When he determines to bring punishment on the wicked, he first uses his representatives on earth to issue warnings, for he is eager to see the wicked do what the Ninevites did—repent and change their ways. (Ezek. 33:11) Jehovah told his prophet Jeremiah: "At any moment that I may speak against a nation and against a kingdom to uproot it and to pull it down and to destroy it, and that nation actually turns back from its badness against which I spoke, I will also feel regret over the calamity that I had thought to execute upon it." —Jer. 18:7, 8.

¹³ Was Jonah's prophecy a false one? No; it fulfilled its purpose as a warning. That warning was based on the Ninevites' bad ways, which subsequently changed. Should the Ninevites resume their wicked ways, God would bring the same judgment against them. That is exactly what happened later on.—Zeph. 2:13-15.

¹⁴ How did Jonah react when destruction did not come at the time he expected it to? We read: "To Jonah, though, it was highly displeasing, and he got to be hot with anger." (Jonah 4:1) Jonah even uttered a prayer that sounds like a rebuke of the Almighty! Jonah suggested that he should have stayed home, on his own ground. He claimed that he knew all along that Jehovah would not bring calamity on Nineveh, even using that as an excuse for his running away to Tarshish in the first place. Then he asked to die, saying that death would be better than life. —*Read Jonah 4:2, 3.*

12, 13. (a) How does Jehovah show that he is reasonable, adaptable, and merciful? (b) Why was Jonah's prophecy not a false one?

14. How did Jonah react to Jehovah's mercy on Nineveh?

Why was Jonah so hot with anger?

15 What was troubling Jonah? We cannot know all that went through his mind, but we do know that Jonah had proclaimed doom to Nineveh before all those people. They had believed him. And now, no doom was coming. Did he fear being ridiculed or being labeled a false prophet? Whatever the case, he did not rejoice over the people's repentance or over Jehovah's mercy. Instead, it seems, he was on a downward spiral into a mire of bitterness, self-pity, and wounded pride. Evidently, though, Jonah's merciful God still saw good in this distressed prophet. Instead of punishing Jonah for his disrespect, Jehovah simply asked him one gentle, probing question: "Have you rightly become hot with anger?" (Jonah 4:4) Did Jonah even answer? The Bible record is silent.

How do we relate to Jonah's reaction?

16 It is easy to judge Jonah for his conduct, but we do well to remember that it is not unusual for imperfect humans to disagree with God. Some may believe that Jehovah should have prevented a tragedy or that he should have executed swift judgment against the wicked or even that he should have brought an end to this whole world system of things before now. Jonah's example serves to remind us that when we disagree with Jehovah God, it is always our own point of view that needs an adjustment —never His.

How Jehovah Taught Jonah a Lesson

17 The despondent prophet left Nineveh and headed, not home, but eastward, where some mountains overlooked the region. He built a little shelter and settled in to wait—and to watch Nineveh. Perhaps he still clung to the hope of witnessing her destruction. How would Jehovah teach this hardheaded man to be merciful?

18 Overnight, Jehovah caused a bottle-gourd plant to sprout up. Jonah woke to see this luxuriant growth, with its broad leaves providing far more shade than his flimsy shelter ever could. His spirits lifted. "Jonah began to rejoice greatly" over the plant, perhaps viewing its miraculous appearance as a sign of God's blessing and approval. However, Jehovah wanted to do more for Jo-

15. (a) What may have led Jonah into a downward spiral? (b) How did Jehovah deal with his distressed prophet?

16. In what ways might some find themselves disagreeing with God, and what lesson can we learn from Jonah's example?

17, 18. (a) What did Jonah do after leaving Nineveh? (b) How did Jehovah's miracles involving a bottle-gourd plant affect Jonah?

nah than simply deliver him from the heat and from his own petulant anger. He wanted to reach Jonah's heart. So God performed additional miracles. He sent a worm to attack and kill the plant. Then he sent "a parching east wind" until Jonah began "swooning away" because of the heat. The man's spirits plummeted, and again he asked God that he might die.—Jonah 4:6-8.

¹⁹ Once more Jehovah asked Jonah if he was rightly angry, this time over the death of the bottle-gourd plant. Instead of repenting, Jonah justified himself, saying: "I have rightly become hot with anger, to the point of death." The stage was now set for Jehovah to drive the lesson home.—Jonah 4:9.

²⁰ God reasoned with Jonah, saying that the prophet was feeling sorry over the death of a mere plant that had sprung up overnight, one that Jonah neither planted nor caused to grow. Then God concluded: "For my part, ought I not to feel sorry for Nineveh the great city, in which there exist more than one

Lesson J taught Jonah.

19, 20. How did Jehovah reason with Jonah about the bottle-gourd plant?

God used the bottle-gourd plant to teach Jonah a lesson in mercy

hundred and twenty thousand men who do not at all know the difference between their right hand and their left, besides many domestic animals?"—Jonah 4:10, 11*

21 Do you see the depth of Jehovah's object lesson? Jonah had never done a thing to take care of that plant. Jehovah, on the other hand, was the Source of life for those Ninevites and had sustained them, as he does all creatures on earth. How could Jonah place more value on a single plant than he did on the lives of 120,000 humans, in addition to all their livestock? Was it not because Jonah had allowed his thinking to become selfish? After all, he felt sorry for the plant only because it had benefited him personally. Did not his anger over Nineveh spring from motives that were likewise selfish—a prideful desire to save face, to be proved right? Jonah's story may help us to take an honest look at ourselves. Who of us is immune to such selfish tendencies? How grateful we should be that Jehovah patiently teaches us to be more selfless, more compassionate, more merciful—as he is!

22 The question is, Did Jonah take the lesson to heart? The book bearing his name ends with Jehovah's question hanging there—in effect, still echoing. Some critics might complain that Jonah never answers. In truth, though, his answer is there. It is the book itself. You see, evidence indicates that Jonah wrote the book bearing his name. Just imagine that prophet, once again safe in his homeland, writing this account. We can almost picture an older, wiser, humbler man ruefully shaking his head as he describes his own mistakes, his rebellion, and his stubborn refusal to show mercy. Clearly, Jonah did learn a vital lesson from Jehovah's wise instruction. He learned to be merciful. Will we? —Read Matthew 5:7.

* God's saying that those people did not know right from left suggested their childlike ignorance of divine standards.

TO THINK ABOUT . . .

• How did Jonah show faith and courage as he preached in Nineveh?

• What can we learn from the Ninevites' repentance?

• What can we learn from Jonah's attitude toward the repentance of the Ninevites?

• In what ways would you like to imitate the faith of Jonah when you receive corrective counsel?

21. (a) What object lesson did Jehovah teach Jonah? (b) How may the account about Jonah help us to take an honest look at ourselves?

22. (a) How was Jonah evidently affected by Jehovah's wise instruction about mercy? (b) What lesson do we all need to learn?

CHAPTER FIFTEEN

She Stood Up for God's People

ESTHER tried to calm her heart as she approached the courtyard in the palace at Shushan. It was not easy. Everything about the castle was designed to inspire awe—its multicolored relief sculptures of winged bulls, archers, and lions of glazed brickwork, its fluted stone columns and imposing statues, even its position atop huge platforms near the snowcapped Zagros Mountains and overlooking the pure waters of the river Choaspes. All of it was intended to remind each visitor of the immense power of the man whom Esther was going to see, the one who called himself "the great king." He was also her husband.

² Husband! How different Ahasuerus was from the kind of husband any faithful Jewish girl might have expected!* He did not look to such examples as Abraham, a man who humbly accepted God's direction to listen to Sarah, his wife. (Gen. 21:12) The king knew little or nothing of Esther's God, Jehovah, or of His Law. Ahasuerus knew Persian law, though, including a law forbidding the very thing that Esther was about to do. What was that? Well, the law said that anyone who appeared before the Persian monarch without first being summoned by the king was liable to death. Esther had not been summoned, but she was going to the king anyway. As she drew near to the inner courtyard, where she would be visible from the king's throne, she may have felt that she was walking to her death.—***Read Esther 4:11; 5:1.***

³ Why did she take such a risk? And what can we learn from the faith of this remarkable woman? First, let us see how Esther got into the unusual position of being a queen in Persia.

---

* Ahasuerus is widely thought to have been Xerxes I, who ruled the Persian Empire early in the fifth century B.C.E.

1-3. (a) Why might Esther have felt intimidated by the prospect of approaching her husband? (b) We will discuss what questions regarding Esther?

Esther's Background

4 Esther was an orphan. We know very little of the parents who named her Hadassah, a Hebrew word for "myrtle," a lovely white-blossomed shrub. When Esther's parents died, one of her relatives, a kindly man named Mordecai, took pity on the child. He was her cousin, but Mordecai was much older. He brought Esther into his home and treated her as his own daughter.—Esther 2:5-7, 15.

5 Mordecai and Esther lived as Jewish exiles in that Persian capital, where they probably had to deal with a measure of disdain because of their religion and the Law they tried to follow. But Esther surely drew closer to her cousin as he taught her about Jehovah, the merciful God who had rescued His people from trouble many times in the past—and would do so again. (Lev. 26: 44, 45) Clearly, a loving and loyal bond grew between Esther and Mordecai.

6 Mordecai evidently worked as some kind of official at the castle at Shushan, regularly sitting within its gate, along with other servants of the king. (Esther 2:19, 21; 3:3) How the young Esther passed her time as she grew up, we can only guess, although it seems safe to say that she took good care of her older cousin and his home, which was likely situated in the humbler quarters across the river from the royal castle. Perhaps she enjoyed going to the market in Shushan, where goldsmiths, silversmiths, and other merchants displayed their wares. Esther could not have imagined that such luxuries would later become commonplace to her; she had no idea of the future in store for her.

"Beautiful in Appearance"

7 One day, Shushan was buzzing with gossip about turmoil in the household of

Mordecai had good reason to be proud of his adopted daughter

4. What was Esther's background, and how did she come to live with her cousin Mordecai?

5, 6. (a) How did Mordecai raise Esther? (b) What kind of life did Esther and Mordecai lead in Shushan?

7. Why was Vashti deposed as queen, and what was the result?

the king. At a grand feast, where Ahasuerus was entertaining his noblemen with sumptuous food and wine, the king decided to summon his beautiful queen, Vashti, who was feasting separately with the women. But Vashti refused to come. Humiliated and enraged, the king asked his advisers how Vashti should be punished. The result? She was deposed as queen. The king's servants began searching throughout the land for beautiful young virgins; from among them the king would select a new queen.—Esther 1: 1–2:4.

⁸ We may imagine Mordecai gazing fondly at Esther from time to time and noting with a mixture of pride and concern that his little cousin was grown-up—and had turned out to be a remarkable beauty. "The young woman was pretty in form and beautiful in appearance," we read. (Esther 2:7) The Bible presents a balanced view of physical beauty—it is delightful, but it needs to be coupled with wisdom and humility. Otherwise, it may breed vanity, pride, and other ugly traits of the heart. (**Read Proverbs 11:22.**) Have you ever seen that to be true? In Esther's case, what would beauty turn out to be—an asset or a liability? Time would tell.

⁹ The king's servants noticed Esther. They gathered her up in their search, taking her away from Mordecai and off to the grand palace across the river. (Esther 2:8) It must have been a difficult parting, for the two were like father and daughter. Mordecai would not have wanted his adopted daughter to marry any unbeliever, even a king, but events were out of his control.* How eagerly Esther must have listened to Mordecai's words of advice before she was taken away! As she was led to Shushan the castle, her mind was filled with questions. What kind of life lay ahead of her?

She Won Favor "in the Eyes of Everyone Seeing Her"

¹⁰ Esther found herself ushered into a world that was entirely new and strange to her. She was among "many young women"

---

* See the box "Questions About Esther," in Chapter 16.

---

8. (a) Why might Mordecai have felt some concern about Esther as she grew up? (b) How do you think we might apply the Bible's balanced view of physical beauty? (See also Proverbs 31:30.)

9. (a) What happened when the king's servants noticed Esther, and why must her parting from Mordecai have been difficult? (b) Why did Mordecai allow Esther to marry a pagan unbeliever? (Include the box.)

10, 11. (a) How might Esther's new environment easily have affected her? (b) How did Mordecai show his concern for Esther's welfare?

who had been gathered from far and wide in the Persian Empire. Their customs, languages, and attitudes must have varied greatly. Placed under the charge of an official named Hegai, the young women were to undergo an extensive beauty treatment, a year-long program that included massages with fragrant oils. (Esther 2:8, 12) Such an environment and lifestyle might easily have bred an obsession with personal appearance among those young women, along with vanity and competitiveness. How was Esther affected?

11 No one on earth could have been more concerned about Esther than Mordecai was. We read that day by day, he made his way as near as he could to the house of the women and endeavored to learn of Esther's welfare. (Esther 2:11) As bits of information trickled out to him, perhaps through cooperative servants

Esther knew that humility and wisdom were far more important than physical appearance

in the household, he must have beamed with fatherly pride. Why?

¹² Esther so impressed Hegai that he treated her with great loving-kindness, giving her seven servant girls and the best place in the house of the women. The account even says: "All the while Esther was continually gaining favor in the eyes of everyone seeing her." (Esther 2:9, 15) Would beauty alone have impressed everyone so profoundly? No, there was much more to Esther than that.

¹³ For instance, we read: "Esther had not told about her people or about her relatives, for Mordecai himself had laid the

---

12, 13. (a) What impression did Esther make on those around her? (b) Why would Mordecai have been pleased to learn that Esther had not revealed her Jewish heritage?

command upon her that she should not tell." (Esther 2:10) Mordecai had instructed the girl to be discreet about her Jewish heritage; he no doubt saw that among Persian royalty, there was much prejudice against his people. What a pleasure it was for him to learn that now, even though Esther was out of his sight, she still showed the same wise and obedient spirit!

¹⁴ Young people today can likewise bring joy to the hearts of parents and guardians. When out of their parents' sight —even if surrounded by people who are shallow, immoral, or vicious—they can resist bad influences and stick to the standards that they know are right. When they do so, like Esther, they make the heart of their heavenly Father rejoice.—*Read Proverbs 27:11.*

¹⁵ When the time came for Esther to be presented to the king, she was given the liberty to select any items that she thought she might need, perhaps to beautify herself further. Modestly, though, she asked for nothing beyond what Hegai mentioned to her. (Esther 2:15) She probably realized that beauty alone would not win the king's heart; a modest and humble spirit would prove a far rarer commodity in that court. Was she right?

¹⁶ The account answers: "The king came to love Esther more than all the other women, so that she gained more favor and loving-kindness before him than all the other virgins. And he proceeded to put the royal headdress upon her head and make her queen instead of Vashti." (Esther 2:17) It must have been hard for this humble Jewish girl to adjust to the change in her life—she was the new queen, wife to the most powerful monarch on earth at that time! Did her new position go to her head, filling her with pride? Far from it!

¹⁷ Esther remained obedient to her adoptive father, Mordecai. She kept her connection to the Jewish people a secret. Further, when Mordecai uncovered a plot to assassinate Ahasuerus, Esther obediently passed his warning along to the king, and the plotters were foiled. (Esther 2:20-23) She still expressed faith in her God by showing a humble, obedient spirit. How we need Es-

14. How can young people today imitate Esther's example?

15, 16. (a) How did Esther win the king's love? (b) Why might the changes in Esther's life have been challenging?

17. (a) In what ways did Esther remain obedient to her adoptive father? (b) Why is Esther's example an important one for us today?

ther's example today, when obedience is rarely valued as a virtue and when disobedience and rebellion are the norm! But people of genuine faith treasure obedience, as Esther did.

Esther's Faith Under Test

18 A man named Haman rose to prominence in the court of Ahasuerus. The king appointed him prime minister, making Haman his principal adviser and the second in command in the empire. The king even decreed that all who saw this official must bow down to him. (Esther 3:1-4) For Mordecai, that law posed a problem. He believed in obeying the king but not at the cost of disrespecting God. You see, Haman was an Agagite. That evidently means that he was a descendant of Agag, the Amalekite king who was executed by God's prophet Samuel. (1 Sam. 15:33) So wicked were the Amalekites that they had made themselves enemies of Jehovah and Israel. As a people, the Amalekites stood condemned by God.* (Deut. 25:19) How could a faithful Jew bow down to an Amalekite? Mordecai could not. He stood his ground. To this day, men and women of faith have risked their lives to adhere to this principle: "We must obey God as ruler rather than men."—Acts 5:29.

19 Haman was enraged. But it was not enough for him to find a way to kill off Mordecai. He wanted to exterminate all of Mordecai's people! Haman persuaded the king by painting a dark portrait of the Jews. Without naming them, he implied that they were inconsequential, a people "scattered and separated among the peoples." Even worse, he said that they did not obey the king's laws; hence, they were dangerous rebels. He proposed to donate to the king's treasury an immense sum of money to cover the expense of slaughtering all the Jews in the empire.# Ahasuerus gave Haman the king's own signet ring to seal any order that he had in mind.—Esther 3:5-10.

* Haman may have been among the very last of the Amalekites, since "the remnant" of them had been destroyed back in the days of King Hezekiah.—1 Chron. 4:43.
# Haman offered 10,000 silver talents, worth hundreds of millions of dollars today. If Ahasuerus was Xerxes I, the money might have made Haman's offer more appealing. Xerxes needed a vast store of funds to carry out his long-proposed but ultimately disastrous war against Greece.

18. (a) Why might Mordecai have refused to bow down to Haman? (See also footnote.) (b) How do men and women of faith today imitate the example of Mordecai?

19. What did Haman want to do, and how did he go about persuading the king?

Esther risked her life to protect God's people

²⁰ Soon messengers were speeding on horseback to every corner of the vast empire, delivering what amounted to a death sentence on the Jewish people. Imagine the impact of such a proclamation when it reached far-off Jerusalem, where a remnant of Jews who had returned from exile in Babylon were struggling to rebuild a city that still had no wall to defend it. Perhaps Mordecai thought of them, as well as of his own friends and relatives in Shushan, when he heard the terrible news. Distraught, he ripped his clothes, wore sackcloth and placed ashes on his head, and cried aloud in the middle of the city. Haman, however, sat drinking with the king, unmoved by the grief he had stirred up among the many Jews and their friends in Shushan.—*Read Esther 3:12–4:1.*

²¹ Mordecai knew that he had to act. But what could he do? Esther heard of his distress and sent clothes to him, but Mordecai refused to take comfort. Maybe he had long wondered why his God, Jehovah, had allowed dear Esther to be taken from him

---

20, 21. (a) How did Haman's proclamation affect the Jews throughout the Persian Empire, including Mordecai? (b) What did Mordecai implore Esther to do?

and made the queen of a pagan ruler. Now the reason seemed to be emerging. Mordecai sent a message to the queen, imploring Esther to intercede with the king, to stand up "for her own people." —Esther 4:4-8.

22 Esther's heart must have sunk when she heard that message. Here was her greatest test of faith. She was afraid, as she freely revealed in her reply to Mordecai. She reminded him of the king's law. To appear before the king unsummoned meant a death sentence. Only if the king held out his golden scepter was the offender spared. And did Esther have any reason to expect such clemency, especially in view of Vashti's fate when she had refused the king's command to appear? Esther told Mordecai that the king had not invited her to see him in 30 days! Such neglect left her plenty of reason to wonder if she had fallen out of favor with this capricious monarch.*—Esther 4:9-11.

23 Mordecai replied firmly to bolster Esther's faith. He assured her that if she failed to act, salvation for the Jews would arise from some other source. But how could she expect to be spared once the persecution gathered force? Here Mordecai showed his profound faith in Jehovah, who would never let His people be exterminated and His promises go unfulfilled. (Josh. 23:14) Then Mordecai asked Esther: "Who is there knowing whether it is for a time like this that you have attained to royal

---

* Xerxes I was known for his mercurial, violent temper. The Greek historian Herodotus recorded some examples from Xerxes' war against Greece. The king ordered that a pontoon bridge of ships be built across the strait of Hellespont. When a storm ruined the bridge, Xerxes ordered the engineers beheaded and even had his men "punish" the Hellespont by whipping the water while an insulting proclamation was read aloud. In the same campaign, when a wealthy man begged that his son be excused from joining the army, Xerxes had the son cut in half, his body displayed as a warning.

---

22. Why was Esther afraid to appear before her husband the king? (See also footnote.)

23. (a) What did Mordecai say to bolster Esther's faith? (b) Why is Mordecai worthy of imitation?

dignity?" (Esther 4:12-14) Is not Mordecai worthy of imitation? He trusted completely in his God, Jehovah. Do we?—Prov. 3:5, 6.

A Faith Stronger Than the Fear of Death

24 For Esther, the time of decision had arrived. She asked Mordecai to get her countrymen to join her in a three-day fast, concluding her message with a statement that resonates down to this day in its simple faith and courage: "In case I must perish, I must perish." (Esther 4:15-17) She must have prayed more fervently in those three days than she ever had in her life. Finally, though, the moment came. She dressed in her very best royal finery, doing all she could to appeal to the king. Then she went.

25 As described at the outset of this chapter, Esther made her way to the king's court. We can only imagine the anxious thoughts and fervent prayers filling her mind and heart. She entered the courtyard, where she could see Ahasuerus on his throne. Perhaps she tried to read the expression on his face—the face that was framed by the carefully tended, symmetrical curls of his hair and of his squared beard. If she had to wait, it must have felt like an eternity. But the moment passed—her husband saw her. He was surely surprised, but his expression softened. He held out his golden scepter!—Esther 5:1, 2.

26 Esther had gained an audience, a hearing ear. She had taken a stand for her God and for her people, setting a beautiful example of faith for all servants of God down through time. True Christians today cherish such examples. Jesus said that his genuine followers would be marked by self-sacrificing love. (**Read John 13:34, 35.**) Showing such love often requires courage like Esther's. But even after Esther stood up for God's people that day, her work was only beginning. How would she convince the king that his favorite adviser, Haman, was a wicked schemer? How could she help to save her people? We will consider these questions in the following chapter.

TO THINK ABOUT . . .

- How did Esther show that she was humble and obedient?
- How did Mordecai help Esther to act faithfully?
- What actions reveal Esther's courage?
- In what ways would you like to imitate the faith of Esther?

---

24. How did Esther show faith and courage?

25. Describe how events unfolded as Esther appeared before her husband.

26. Why do true Christians need courage like Esther's, and why was her work only beginning?

CHAPTER SIXTEEN

She Acted Wisely, Bravely, and Selflessly

ESTHER slowly approached the throne, her heart racing. Imagine a hush falling over the great royal chamber in the Persian palace of Shushan, a silence so profound that Esther could hear her own soft footsteps and the rustling of her royal garments. She could not let her attention wander to the grandeur of the royal court, the graceful columns, the richly carved ceiling of cedars imported from distant Lebanon. She trained all her attention on the man seated on the throne, the man who held her life in his hands.

2 The king watched intently as Esther approached, extending his golden scepter toward her. It was a simple gesture, but it meant Esther's life, for by it the king excused her from the offense she had just committed—that of appearing before him without a royal invitation. As she came to the throne, Esther reached out and gratefully touched the top of the scepter.—Esther 5:1, 2.

3 Everything about King Ahasuerus bespoke his immense wealth and power. The royal garb of the Persian monarchs of those times reputedly cost the equivalent of hundreds of millions of dollars. Yet, Esther could see some warmth in her husband's eyes; in his own way, he did love her. He said: "What do you have, O Esther the queen, and what is your request? To the half of the kingship—let it even be given to you!"—Esther 5:3.

4 Esther had already shown remarkable faith and courage; she had come before the king to protect her people from a plot to wipe them all out. So far, she had met with success, but greater challenges lay ahead. She had to convince this proud monarch that his most trusted adviser was a wicked man who

---

1-3. (a) What was it like for Esther to approach her husband's throne? (b) How did the king respond to Esther's visit?

4. What challenges lay ahead of Esther?

had duped him into condemning Esther's people to death. How would she persuade him, and what can we learn from her faith?

She Wisely Chose "a Time to Speak"

5 Should Esther have revealed to the king the whole problem in front of his court? Doing so might have humiliated him and given his adviser Haman time to dispute her charges. So, what did Esther do? Centuries earlier, wise King Solomon was inspired to write: "For everything there is an appointed time, . . . a time to keep quiet and a time to speak." (Eccl. 3:1, 7) We may imagine Esther's adoptive father, the faithful man Mordecai, teaching the young woman such principles as she grew up under his care. Esther certainly understood the importance of choosing carefully the "time to speak."

5, 6. (a) How did Esther apply the principle found at Ecclesiastes 3:1, 7? (b) How did Esther's way of approaching her husband prove wise?

⁶ Esther said: "If to the king it does seem good, let the king with Haman come today to the banquet that I have made for him." (Esther 5:4) The king agreed and had Haman summoned. Can you see how wisely Esther spoke? She preserved her husband's dignity and created a more suitable setting for revealing her concerns to him.—*Read Proverbs 10:19.*

⁷ No doubt Esther prepared that feast carefully, seeing to it that in every detail she catered to her husband's preferences. The banquet included fine wine to encourage a happy mood. (Ps. 104:15) Ahasuerus enjoyed himself, and he was moved to ask Esther again what her petition might be. Was this now the time to speak?

⁸ Esther thought not. Rather, she invited the king and Haman to come to a second banquet, on the following day. (Esther 5:7, 8) Why did she delay? Remember, all of Esther's people were

7, 8. What was Esther's first banquet like, yet why did she delay in speaking up to the king?

137

facing death by the king's decree. With so much at stake, Esther had to be sure that the time was right. So she waited, creating yet another opportunity to show her husband how highly she regarded him.

⁹ Patience is a rare and precious quality. Though distressed and eager to speak her mind, Esther patiently waited for the right moment. We can learn much from her example, for all of us have likely seen wrongs that need to be put right. If we seek to convince someone in authority to address a problem, we may need to imitate Esther and be patient. Proverbs 25:15 says: "By patience a commander is induced, and a mild tongue itself can break a bone." If we wait patiently for the right moment and speak mildly, as Esther did, even opposition as hard as bone may be broken. Did Esther's God, Jehovah, bless her patience and wisdom?

---

9. What is the value of patience, and how can we imitate Esther's example in this regard?

Questions About Esther

Why did Mordecai allow Esther to marry a pagan unbeliever?

There is no basis for the suggestion of some scholars that Mordecai was an opportunist who wanted Esther to wed the king for the sake of prestige. As a faithful Jew, he would not have favored such a marriage. (Deut. 7:3) Ancient Jewish tradition holds that Mordecai tried to prevent the marriage. It seems unlikely that either he or Esther, mere foreigners in a land ruled by an autocrat who held a godlike status, would have had much choice in the matter. In time, it became clear that Jehovah used Esther's marriage as a means of protecting his people.—Esther 4:14.

Why does the book of Esther contain no mention of God's personal name, Jehovah?

Mordecai was evidently the inspired writer of the book. Perhaps the book was at first kept with official Persian records before it was taken to Jerusalem. The use of Jehovah's name might have moved worshippers of the Persian gods to destroy the book. In any case, Jehovah's involvement in the story is clear. Interestingly, God's personal name is contained in the original Hebrew text by means of acrostics, wherein the phrasing appears to have been arranged deliberately so that the first or the last letters of successive words spell out God's name.—Esther 1:20, ftn.

Is the book of Esther historically inaccurate?

Critics level that charge against the book. However, some scholars have noted that the writer of the book showed a remarkably detailed knowledge of Persian royalty, architecture, and customs. True, no mention of Queen Esther has been found in surviving secular documents, but Esther would hardly be the only royal personage who was erased from public records. What is more, secular records do show that a man named *Mardukâ*, a Persian equivalent of Mordecai, served as a court official in Shushan at the time described in the book.

Patience Paves the Way for Justice

10 Esther's patience paved the way for a remarkable chain of events. Haman left the first banquet in high spirits, "joyful and merry of heart" that the king and queen favored him so. As Haman passed through the castle gate, though, his eyes fell on Mordecai, that Jew who still refused to pay him special homage. As we noted in the preceding chapter, Mordecai's reasons had nothing to do with disrespect but, rather, with his conscience and his relationship with Jehovah God. Yet, Haman "was immediately filled with rage."—Esther 5:9.

11 When Haman told his wife and friends of this slight, they urged him to prepare a huge stake, over 72 feet tall, and then to ask the king's permission to hang Mordecai on it. Haman liked their idea and immediately set about the task.—Esther 5:12-14.

12 Meanwhile, the king had an unusual night. "The king's sleep fled," the Bible tells us, so he had the official records of State read aloud to him. The reading included the report of an assassination plot against Ahasuerus. He remembered the affair; the would-be murderers were caught and executed. What, though, about the man who had exposed the plot—Mordecai? Suddenly alert, the king asked how Mordecai had been rewarded. The answer? Nothing at all had been done for the man. —*Read Esther 6:1-3.*

13 Agitated, the king asked what court officials were available to help him correct this oversight. Of all people, Haman was in the king's court—early, it seems, because he was eager to secure permission to execute Mordecai. But before Haman could make his request, the king asked him how best to honor a man who had won the king's favor. Haman assumed that the king had him in mind. So Haman devised a lavish honor: Clothe the man in royal garb, and have a high official parade him around Shushan on the king's own horse, calling out the man's praises for all to hear. Imagine the expression on Haman's face when he learned that the man to be honored was Mordecai! And whom did the king assign to sing out Mordecai's praises? Haman!—Esther 6: 4-10.

10, 11. Why did Haman's mood change after he left the first banquet, and what did his wife and friends urge him to do?

12. Why did the king have the official records of State read aloud to him, and what did he learn as a result?

13, 14. (a) How did things start to go wrong for Haman? (b) What did Haman's wife and friends tell him?

Esther bravely pointed out the wickedness of Haman

¹⁴ Haman grudgingly carried out what to him was an odious duty and then rushed home in distress. His wife and friends said that this turn of events could only bode ill; he was bound to fail in his fight against Mordecai the Jew.—Esther 6:12, 13.

¹⁵ Because Esther was patient, waiting that one extra day to present her request to the king, Haman was given time to lay the basis for his own downfall. And might not Jehovah God have been behind the king's sleeplessness? (Prov. 21:1) Little wonder that God's Word encourages us to show "a waiting attitude"! (*Read Micah 7:7.*) When we wait on God, we may find that his solutions to our problems far exceed anything that we might have devised ourselves.

She Spoke Up Bravely

¹⁶ Esther dared not test the king's patience any further; at her second banquet, she had to tell all. But how? As it turned out, the king gave her the opportunity, asking again what her petition might be. (Esther 7:2) Esther's "time to speak" had come.

¹⁷ We may imagine Esther saying a silent prayer to her God before uttering these words: "If I have found favor in your eyes, O king, and if to the king it does seem good, let there be given me my own soul at my petition and my people at my request." (Esther 7:3) Notice that she assured the king that she respected

15. (a) What good came of Esther's patience? (b) Why is it wise for us to show "a waiting attitude"?

16, 17. (a) When did Esther's "time to speak" come? (b) How did Esther differ from Vashti, the king's former wife?

140

his judgment regarding what seemed good. How Esther differed from Vashti, the king's former wife, who had purposely humiliated her husband! (Esther 1:10-12) Further, Esther did not criticize the king for his folly of trusting in Haman. Rather, she begged the king to protect her from a danger to her own life.

18 That request surely moved and amazed the king. Who would dare endanger his queen? Esther went on: "We have been sold, I and my people, to be annihilated, killed and destroyed. Now if we had been sold for mere men slaves and for mere maidservants, I should have kept silent. But the distress is not appropriate when with damage to the king." (Esther 7:4) Note that Esther frankly exposed the problem, yet she added that she would have kept quiet about it if mere slavery had been the threat. This genocide, though, would be too costly to the king himself to keep quiet about it.

19 Esther's example teaches us much about the art of persuasion. If you ever need to lay bare a serious problem to a loved one or even to a person in authority, a combination of patience, respect, and candor can be of great help.—Prov. 16:21, 23.

20 Ahasuerus demanded: "Who is this, and just where is the one who has emboldened himself to do that way?" Imagine Esther pointing a finger as she said: "The man, the adversary and enemy, is this bad Haman." The accusation hung in the

18. How did Esther reveal the problem to the king?
19. What can we learn from Esther about the art of persuasion?
20, 21. (a) How did Esther expose Haman, eliciting what reaction from the king? (b) How did Haman act when exposed as a scheming coward?

A Prophecy Fulfilled

In fighting for God's people, Esther and Mordecai fulfilled an ancient Bible prophecy. Over a dozen centuries earlier, Jehovah inspired the patriarch Jacob to foretell regarding one of his sons: "Benjamin will keep on tearing like a wolf. In the morning he will eat the animal seized and at evening he will divide spoil." (Gen. 49:27) In "the morning" of Israel's kingly history, Benjamin's descendants included King Saul and other mighty warriors for Jehovah's people. In the "evening" of that royal history, after the sun had set on Israel's kingly line, Esther and Mordecai, both of the tribe of Benjamin, warred effectively against Jehovah's enemies. In a sense, they also divided spoil, in that Haman's vast estate went to them.

air. Terror filled Haman. Picture the volatile monarch's face coloring as he realized that his trusted adviser had duped him into signing an order that would destroy his own beloved wife! The king stormed out into the garden to regain his composure.—Esther 7:5-7.

21 Haman, exposed as the scheming coward that he was, groveled at the queen's feet. When the king came back into the room and saw Haman on Esther's couch pleading with her, he angrily accused Haman of attempting to rape the queen in the king's own home. That sounded the death knell for Haman. He was taken away, his face covered. One of the king's officials then spoke up, telling the king of the huge stake that Haman had intended for Mordecai. Ahasuerus immediately ordered that Haman himself be hanged on it.—Esther 7:8-10.

22 In today's unjust world, it is easy to imagine that we will never see justice done. Have you ever felt that way? Esther never despaired, never turned cynical, never lost faith. When the time came, she spoke up bravely for what was right, and she trusted in Jehovah to do the rest. Let us do the same! Jehovah has not changed since Esther's day. He is still more than able to catch the wicked and cunning in their own traps, just as he did Haman.—*Read Psalm 7:11-16.*

She Acted Unselfishly for Jehovah and for His People

23 At last, the king learned who Mordecai was—not only his loyal protector against assassination but also the adoptive father of Esther. Ahasuerus bestowed Haman's position as prime minister on Mordecai. Haman's house—including his immense fortune—the king gave to Esther, who placed Mordecai over it.—Esther 8:1, 2.

---

22. How can Esther's example teach us never to despair, turn cynical, or lose faith?

23. (a) How did the king reward Mordecai and Esther? (b) How was Jacob's deathbed prophecy over Benjamin fulfilled? (See the box "A Prophecy Fulfilled.")

24 Now that Esther and Mordecai were safe, could the queen relax? Only if she were selfish. At that moment, Haman's decree to kill all the Jews was making its way to every corner of the empire. Haman had cast lots, or *Pur*—evidently a form of spiritism—to determine the opportune time to carry out this vicious attack. (Esther 9:24-26) The day was yet months away, but it was fast approaching. Could disaster still be averted?

25 Esther unselfishly risked her life again, appearing before the king once more without an official invitation. This time, she wept for her people, pleading with her husband to revoke the terrible edict. But laws passed in the Persian monarch's name could not be revoked. (Dan. 6:12, 15) So the king empowered Esther and Mordecai to enact a new law. A second proclamation was sent out, giving the Jews the right to defend themselves. Riders sped to every part of the empire, taking this good news to the Jews. Hope was kindled anew in many hearts. (Esther 8:3-16) We may imagine the Jews throughout that vast empire arming themselves and preparing for battle, which they could never have done without that new edict. More important, though, would "Jehovah of armies" be with his people?—1 Sam. 17:45.

24, 25. (a) Why could Esther not relax after Haman's plot was exposed? (b) How did Esther risk her life once more?

Esther and Mordecai sent out proclamations to the Jews of the Persian Empire

26 When the chosen day finally came, God's people were ready. Even many Persian officials were on their side now, as news had traveled far and wide about the new prime minister, Mordecai the Jew. Jehovah gave his people a great victory. He no doubt protected his people from terrible reprisals by handing their enemies a thorough defeat.*—Esther 9:1-6.

27 Furthermore, Mordecai would never be safe to preside over Haman's house while the ten sons of that evil man still lived. They too were killed. (Esther 9:7-10) A Bible prophecy was thus fulfilled, for God had earlier foretold the complete destruction of the Amalekites, who had proved to be wicked enemies of his people. (Deut. 25:17-19) The sons of Haman may well have been among the very last of that condemned nation.

28 Esther had to take on her young shoulders her share of very heavy burdens—such as royal edicts involving war and execution. It could not have been easy. But Jehovah's will required that his people be protected from destruction; the nation of Israel was to produce the promised Messiah, the one source of hope for all mankind! (Gen. 22:18) Servants of God today are delighted to know that when the Messiah, Jesus, came to the earth, he forbade his followers from that time forward to take part in physical warfare.—Matt. 26:52.

29 Nonetheless, Christians do engage in spiritual warfare; Satan is ever more eager to destroy our faith in Jehovah God. (**Read 2 Corinthians 10:3, 4.**) What a blessing to have Esther as an example! Like her, may we show faith by our wise and patient use of persuasion, by our courage, and by our unselfish willingness to stand up for God's people.

TO THINK ABOUT . . .

- How did Esther show wisdom in choosing "a time to speak"?
- Esther's patience led to what blessings?
- How did Esther prove to be brave and selfless in defending her people?
- In what ways are you determined to imitate the faith of Esther?

* The king allowed the Jews a second day to finish their conquest of their enemies. (Esther 9:12-14) Even today, the Jews commemorate that victory each year in the month of Adar, which corresponds to late February and early March. The festival is called Purim, named after the lots that Haman cast in his quest to destroy Israel.

26, 27. (a) How great and how thorough was the victory that Jehovah gave his people over their enemies? (b) What prophecy was fulfilled by the destruction of Haman's sons?

28, 29. (a) Why was it Jehovah's will for Esther and her people to be involved in warfare? (b) Why is Esther's example a blessing for us today?

CHAPTER SEVENTEEN

"Look! Jehovah's Slave Girl!"

MARY looked up, wide-eyed, as the visitor entered her home. He did not ask for her father or her mother. He was there to see her! He could not be from Nazareth; of that she was sure. In a small town like hers, strangers stood out. This one would stand out anywhere. He addressed Mary in a way that was altogether new to her, saying: "Good day, highly favored one, Jehovah is with you."—*Read Luke 1:26-28.*

2 Thus the Bible introduces us to Mary, daughter of Heli, of the town of Nazareth in Galilee. We meet her at a crossroads, in a sense. She was engaged to marry the carpenter Joseph who was, not a man of wealth, but a man of faith. So her course may have seemed to lie neatly mapped out before her—a simple life of working supportively as the wife of Joseph, raising a family together with him. Suddenly, though, she found herself faced with this visitor who brought her an assignment from her God, a responsibility that would change her life.

3 Many are surprised to learn that the Bible does not tell us much about Mary. It says little of her background, less of her personality, and nothing at all of her appearance. Yet, what God's Word does say about her is revealing indeed.

4 In order to get acquainted with Mary, we need to look beyond many preconceptions about her that are promoted in various religions. So let us ignore the countless "likenesses" executed in paint, marble, or plaster. Let us ignore, too, the complex theology and dogma that bestow on this humble woman such lofty titles as "Mother of God" and "Queen of Heaven." Let us instead focus on what the Bible actually reveals. It gives us priceless insight into her faith and how we can imitate it.

1, 2. (a) Mary received what greeting from a stranger? (b) In what way was Mary at a crossroads?

3, 4. In order to get acquainted with Mary, what do we need to ignore, and on what do we need to focus?

A Visit From an Angel

5 Mary's visitor was no mere man. It was the angel Gabriel. When he called Mary "highly favored one," she was "deeply disturbed" by his words and wondered about this unusual greeting. (Luke 1:29) Highly favored by whom? Mary did not expect to be highly favored among men. But the angel was speaking of the favor of Jehovah God. That mattered to her. Still, she did not proudly presume that she had God's favor. If we strive for God's favor, never haughtily assuming that we already have it, we will learn a vital lesson that young Mary fully understood. God opposes the haughty, but he loves and supports the lowly and humble.—Jas. 4:6.

6 Mary would need such humility, for the angel held out to her an almost unimaginable privilege. He explained that she was to bear a child who would become the most important of all humans. Gabriel said: "Jehovah God will give him the throne of David his father, and he will rule as king over the house of Jacob forever, and there will be no end of his kingdom." (Luke 1: 32, 33) Mary surely knew of the promise God had made to David more than one thousand years earlier—namely, that one of his descendants would rule forever. (2 Sam. 7:12, 13) So her son would be the Messiah whom God's people over the centuries had been hoping for!

> Mary did not proudly presume that she had God's favor

7 What is more, the angel told her that her son would "be called Son of the Most High." How could a human woman produce God's Son? Really, how could Mary produce a son at all? She was engaged to Joseph but not yet married to him. This question Mary put into frank words: "How is this to be, since I am having no intercourse with a man?" (Luke 1:34) Note that Mary spoke of her virginity without a trace of shame. On the contrary, she treasured her chastity. Today, many youths are eager to cast off their virginity and quick to ridicule those who do not. The world has certainly changed. Jehovah, however, has not

5. (a) What can we learn about Mary from her reaction to Gabriel's greeting? (b) What vital lesson can we learn from Mary?

6. The angel held out what privilege to Mary?

7. (a) What did Mary's question reveal about her? (b) What can young people today learn from Mary?

The angel Gabriel held out to Mary an almost unimaginable privilege

changed. (Mal. 3:6) As in Mary's day, he values those who adhere to his moral standards.—*Read Hebrews 13:4.*

8 Although she was a faithful servant of God, Mary was an imperfect human. How, then, could she produce a perfect offspring, the Son of God? Gabriel explained: "Holy spirit will come upon you, and power of the Most High will overshadow you. For that reason also what is born will be called holy, God's Son." (Luke 1:35) Holy means "clean," "pure," "sacred." Normally, humans pass on their unclean, sinful state to their offspring. In this case, though, Jehovah would perform a unique miracle. He would transfer the life of his Son from heaven to the womb of Mary and then use his active force, or holy spirit, to "overshadow" Mary, shielding the child from any taint of sin. Did Mary believe the angel's promise? How did she respond?

Mary's Response to Gabriel

9 Skeptics, including some theologians of Christendom, have a hard time believing that a virgin could give birth. For all their education, they fail to grasp a simple truth. As Gabriel put it, "with God no declaration will be an impossibility." (Luke 1: 37) Mary accepted Gabriel's words as truth, for she was a young woman of great faith. However, that faith was not gullibility. Like any reasoning person, Mary needed evidence on which to base her faith. Gabriel was prepared to add to her store of such evidence. He told her about her elderly relative Elizabeth, long known as a barren woman. God had miraculously enabled her to conceive!

10 Now what would Mary do? She had her assignment before her and had evidence that God was going to do all that Gabriel had said. We should not assume that this privilege presented no fears, no hardships. For one thing, she had her engagement to Joseph to consider. Would their marriage proceed when he found out about her pregnancy? For another thing, the assignment itself may have seemed a daunting responsibility. She was to carry the life of the most precious of all of God's creatures—his own beloved Son! She would have to care

8. How could Mary, though imperfect, produce a perfect offspring?

9. (a) Why are skeptics wrong to doubt the account about Mary? (b) In what way did Gabriel strengthen Mary's faith?

10. Why should we not assume that Mary's privilege presented no fears or hardships?

for him when he was a helpless infant and protect him in a wicked world. A weighty responsibility indeed!

11 The Bible shows that even strong, faithful men have sometimes hesitated to accept challenging assignments from God. Moses protested that he could not speak fluently enough to act as God's spokesman. (Ex. 4:10) Jeremiah objected that he was "but a boy," too young to take on the task God had assigned him. (Jer. 1:6) And Jonah ran away from his assignment! (Jonah 1:3) What about Mary?

12 Her words, so full of simple humility and obedience, resonate for all people of faith. She said to Gabriel: "Look! Jehovah's slave girl! May it take place with me according to your declaration." (Luke 1:38) A slave girl was the lowliest of servants; her life was entirely in the hands of her master. That is how Mary felt about her Master, Jehovah. She knew that she was safe in his hands, that he is loyal to those who are loyal to him, and that he would bless her as she did her best with this challenging assignment.—Ps. 18:25.

Mary knew that she was safe in the hands of her loyal God, Jehovah

13 Sometimes God asks us to do what may seem difficult, even impossible, in our eyes. However, in his Word he gives us ample reasons to trust him, to place ourselves in his hands, as Mary did. (Prov. 3:5, 6) Will we? If we do, he will reward us, giving us reasons to build even stronger faith in him.

The Visit With Elizabeth

14 Gabriel's words about Elizabeth meant a lot to Mary. Of all the women in the world, who could understand her situation better? Mary hurried to the mountainous country of Judah, a trip of perhaps three or four days. As she entered the home of Elizabeth and Zechariah the priest, Jehovah rewarded Mary with further solid evidence to bolster her faith. Elizabeth heard Mary's

---

11, 12. (a) How have even strong, faithful men sometimes responded to challenging assignments from God? (b) What did Mary reveal about herself in her response to Gabriel?

13. If doing what God asks of us seems difficult or even impossible, how can we benefit from Mary's example?

14, 15. (a) How did Jehovah reward Mary when she visited Elizabeth and Zechariah? (b) What does Mary's speech recorded at Luke 1:46-55 reveal about her?

greeting and immediately felt the infant in her womb leap for joy. She was filled with holy spirit and spoke of Mary as "the mother of my Lord." God had revealed to Elizabeth that Mary's son would become her Lord, the Messiah. Further, she was inspired to commend Mary for her faithful obedience, saying: "Happy too is she that believed." (Luke 1:39-45) Yes, everything that Jehovah had promised Mary would come true!

The friendship of Mary and Elizabeth was a blessing to them both

15 In turn, Mary spoke. Her words are carefully preserved in God's Word. (*Read Luke 1:46-55.*) It is by far Mary's longest speech in the Bible record, and it reveals much about her. It shows her thankful, appreciative spirit as she praises Jehovah for

blessing her with the privilege of serving as the mother of the Messiah. It shows the depth of her faith as she speaks of Jehovah as abasing the haughty and powerful and as helping the lowly and poor who seek to serve him. It also hints at the extent of her knowledge. By one estimate, she made over 20 references to the Hebrew Scriptures!*

16 Clearly, Mary thought deeply about God's Word. Still, she remained humble, preferring to let the Scriptures do the talking rather than speaking of her own originality. The son who was then growing in her womb would one day show the same spirit, saying: "What I teach is not mine, but belongs to him that sent me." (John 7:16) We do well to ask ourselves: 'Do I show such respect and reverence for God's Word? Or do I prefer my own ideas and teachings?' Mary's position is clear.

17 Mary remained with Elizabeth for about three months, no doubt receiving and providing a great deal of encouragement. (Luke 1:56) The Bible's warm account of this visit reminds us of what a blessing friendship can be. If we seek out friends who truly love our God, Jehovah, we are sure to grow spiritually and draw closer to him. (Prov. 13:20) Finally, though, it was time for Mary to return home. What would Joseph say when he learned of her condition?

Mary and Joseph

18 Mary likely did not wait for her pregnancy to reveal itself. She no doubt had to speak to Joseph. Beforehand, she may have wondered how this decent, God-fearing man would respond to what she had to tell him. Nonetheless, she approached him and told him all that had happened to her. As you might imagine, Joseph was deeply troubled. He wanted to believe this dear girl, but it seemed that she had been unfaithful to him. The Bible does not say what thoughts went through his mind or how he reasoned. But it does say that he decided to divorce her, for at that time, engaged couples were viewed as being married. However, he did not want to expose her to public shame and scandal, so he chose to divorce her in secret. (Matt. 1:18, 19) It must

---

* Among such references, Mary evidently quoted from the faithful woman Hannah, who had also received a blessing from Jehovah in the matter of childbirth.—See the box "Two Remarkable Prayers," in Chapter 6.

16, 17. (a) How did Mary and her son show a spirit that we need to imitate? (b) Mary's visit with Elizabeth reminds us of what blessing?

18. What did Mary reveal to Joseph, and how did he respond?

have pained Mary to see this kind man agonizing over this unprecedented situation. Yet, Mary was not embittered.

19 Jehovah kindly helped Joseph to find the best course. In a dream, God's angel told him that Mary's pregnancy was indeed miraculous. That must have been a relief! Joseph now did what Mary had done from the start—he acted in harmony with Jehovah's leading. He took Mary as his wife, and he prepared to take on the unique responsibility of caring for Jehovah's Son. —Matt. 1:20-24.

20 Married people—and those contemplating marriage—do well to learn from this young couple of 2,000 years ago. As Joseph saw his young wife fulfill the duties and cares of motherhood, he was surely pleased that Jehovah's angel had directed him. Joseph must have seen the importance of leaning on Jehovah when making major decisions. (Ps. 37:5; Prov. 18:13) He no doubt remained careful and kind in making decisions as the family head.

21 On the other hand, what can we surmise from Mary's willingness to marry Joseph? Although at first he may have found her story difficult to comprehend, she waited on him to decide how to proceed, for he was the man who would be the family head. That certainly was a good lesson for her, as it is for Christian women today. Finally, these incidents likely taught both Joseph and Mary much about the value of honest and open communication.—*Read Proverbs 15:22.*

22 That young couple certainly started their marriage off on the best of foundations. They both loved Jehovah God above all and yearned to please him as responsible, caring parents. Of course, greater blessings awaited them—and greater challenges too. Before them lay the prospect of raising Jesus, who would grow up to be the greatest man the world has ever known.

TO THINK ABOUT . . .
- What can we learn from Mary about humility?
- How was Mary's obedience outstanding?
- In what ways did Mary strengthen her faith?
- In what ways would you like to imitate the faith of Mary?

19. How did Jehovah help Joseph to follow the best course?

20, 21. What can married people and those contemplating marriage learn from Mary and Joseph?

22. What was the foundation of Joseph and Mary's marriage, and what prospect lay before them?

CHAPTER EIGHTEEN

She Drew "Conclusions in Her Heart"

MARY shifted her weight uncomfortably atop the little beast of burden. She had been riding for hours. Just ahead, Joseph walked steadily onward, leading the way along the road toward distant Bethlehem. Mary once again felt the stirring of life within her.

² Mary was well along in her pregnancy; the Bible describes her at this time with the expressive phrase "heavy with child." (Luke 2:5) As the couple passed by one field after another, perhaps some of the farmers looked up from their plowing or sowing and wondered why a woman in such a condition would go on a journey. What had led Mary so far from her home in Nazareth?

³ It all began months earlier when this young Jewish woman received an assignment that was unique in all human history. She was to give birth to the child who would become the Messiah, the Son of God! (Luke 1:35) As the time to give birth approached, the need to take this journey arose. In the process, Mary faced a number of challenges to her faith. Let us see what helped her to stay spiritually strong.

The Trip to Bethlehem

⁴ Joseph and Mary were not the only ones on the move. Caesar Augustus had recently decreed that a registration be carried out in the land, and people had to travel to their town of origin in order to comply. How did Joseph respond? The account reads: "Of course, Joseph also went up from Galilee, out of the city of Nazareth, into Judea, to David's city, which is called Bethlehem,

1, 2. Describe Mary's journey, and explain what made it uncomfortable for her.

3. What assignment had Mary received, and what will we seek to learn about her?

4, 5. (a) Why were Joseph and Mary heading to Bethlehem? (b) Caesar's decree led to the fulfillment of what prophecy?

because of his being a member of the house and family of David."—Luke 2:1-4.

⁵ It was no coincidence that Caesar issued his decree at this time. A prophecy written down some seven centuries earlier foretold that the Messiah would be born in Bethlehem. Now, it so happened that there was a town named Bethlehem a mere seven miles from Nazareth. However, the prophecy specified that it was "Bethlehem Ephrathah" that would produce the Messiah. (*Read Micah 5:2.*) To reach that little village from Nazareth, travelers covered some 80 hilly miles via Samaria. That was the Bethlehem to which Joseph was summoned, for it was the ancestral home of the family of King David—the family to which both Joseph and his bride belonged.

⁶ Would Mary support Joseph in his decision to comply? After all, the trip would be hard on her. It was likely early in the autumn of the year, so light rains were possible as the dry season gradually ended. What is more, the phrase "went *up* from Galilee" is appropriate, for Bethlehem was perched at a lofty altitude of over 2,500 feet—quite a climb, an arduous end to a trek of several days. Perhaps it would take longer than usual, for

---

6, 7. (a) Why might a journey to Bethlehem have presented challenges to Mary? (b) Being the wife of Joseph made what difference in Mary's decisions? (See also footnote.)

Mary's condition might require numerous periods of rest. Now, of all times, a young woman might yearn to stay close to home, where she had family and friends who were ready to help when her birth pangs began. Without a doubt, she needed to have courage to take this trip.

⁷ Nonetheless, Luke writes that Joseph went "to get registered with Mary." He also notes that Mary "had been given [to Joseph] in marriage as promised." (Luke 2:4, 5) Being Joseph's wife made a great deal of difference in Mary's decisions. She viewed her husband as her spiritual head, embracing her God-given role as his helper by supporting him in his decisions.* So she met this potential challenge to her faith with simple obedience.

⁸ What else may have motivated Mary to obey? Did she know of the prophecy about Bethlehem as the birthplace of the Messiah? The Bible does not say. We cannot rule out the possibility, for the fact was evidently common knowledge among religious leaders and even people in general. (Matt. 2:1-7; John 7:

---

* Note the contrast between this passage and the description of an earlier trip: "Mary rose . . . and went" to visit Elizabeth. (Luke 1:39) At that time, as an engaged but unwed woman, Mary may have acted without consulting Joseph. After the couple were married, the action of their trip together is ascribed to Joseph, not Mary.

---

8. (a) What else may have motivated Mary to go to Bethlehem with Joseph? (b) In what way is Mary's example a beacon for faithful people?

The journey to Bethlehem was not an easy one

40-42) When it came to the Scriptures, Mary was far from an ignorant girl. (Luke 1:46-55) At any rate, whether Mary decided to travel in order to obey her husband, a secular decree, or Jehovah's own prophecy—or because of a combination of factors—she set a splendid example. Jehovah greatly values a humble, obedient spirit in both men and women. In our age, when submission often seems to be among the most disregarded of virtues, Mary's example stands as a beacon for faithful people everywhere.

The Birth of Christ

9 Mary must have breathed a sigh of relief when she first caught sight of Bethlehem. As they mounted the hillsides, passing by olive groves—among the last of the crops to be harvested—Mary and Joseph may well have thought about the history of this little village. It was too insignificant to be numbered among Judah's cities, just as Micah the prophet had said; yet it was the birthplace of Boaz, Naomi, and later David, all more than a thousand years earlier.

10 Mary and Joseph found the village to be crowded. Others had arrived to register before them, so there was no space for them at the lodging room.* They had no choice but to settle down for the night in a stable. We can just imagine Joseph's concern as he saw his wife suffering a sharp discomfort she had never known, which then intensified. Here, of all places, her birth pangs had begun.

11 Women everywhere can empathize with Mary. Some 4,000 years earlier, Jehovah had foretold that it would be the common lot of women to suffer pain during childbirth because of inherited sin. (Gen. 3:16) There is no evidence to suggest that Mary was any exception. Luke's account draws a discreet curtain of privacy around the scene, saying simply: "She gave birth to her son, the firstborn." (Luke 2:7) Yes, her "firstborn" had arrived —the first of Mary's many children, at least seven in all. (Mark 6:3) This one, though, would ever stand apart. Not only was he *her* firstborn but he was Jehovah's own "firstborn of all creation," the only-begotten Son of God!—Col. 1:15.

---

* It was the practice of the day for towns to provide a common room to shelter travelers and passing caravans.

9, 10. (a) What might Mary and Joseph have thought about while approaching Bethlehem? (b) Why did Joseph and Mary lodge where they did?

11. (a) Why can women everywhere empathize with Mary? (b) In what ways was Jesus a "firstborn"?

[12] It is at this point that the account adds a famous detail: "She bound him with cloth bands and laid him in a manger." (Luke 2:7) Nativity plays, paintings, and scenes around the world sentimentalize this setting. Consider, though, the reality. A manger is a feeding trough, a bin from which farm animals eat. Remember, the family was lodging in a stable, hardly a place to be noted for good air or hygiene—then or now. Really, what parents would choose such a spot for childbirth if there were any other options? Most parents want the best for their children. How much more so did Mary and Joseph want to provide the best for the Son of God!

[13] However, they did not let their limitations embitter them; they simply did the best they could with what they had. Notice, for instance, that Mary herself cared for the infant, wrapping him up snugly in cloth bands, then laying him carefully in the manger to sleep, ensuring that he would be warm and safe. Mary was not about to let anxiety over her present circumstances distract her from providing the best that she could. She and Joseph both knew, too, that caring spiritually for this child would be the most important thing they could do for him. (**Read Deuteronomy 6: 6-8.**) Today, wise parents cultivate similar priorities as they bring their children up in this spiritually impoverished world.

A Visit Brings Encouragement

[14] A sudden commotion disturbed the peaceful scene. Shepherds rushed into the stable, eager to see the family and the child in particular. These men were bubbling over with excitement, their faces radiating joy. They had hurried in from the hillsides where they were living with their flocks.* They told the wondering parents about a marvelous experience they had just had. On the hillside during the night watch, an angel had suddenly appeared to them. Jehovah's glory had gleamed all around, and the

---

* That these shepherds at the time were living out-of-doors with their flocks confirms what Bible chronology indicates: The birth of Christ did not occur in December when the flocks would have been sheltered closer to home but, rather, sometime in early October.

---

12. Where did Mary lay the baby, and how was the reality different from nativity plays, paintings, and scenes?

13. (a) In what way did Mary and Joseph do their best with what they had? (b) How can wise parents today cultivate priorities similar to those of Joseph and Mary?

14, 15. (a) Why were the shepherds eager to see the child? (b) What did the shepherds do about what they had seen in the stable?

angel told them that the Christ, or Messiah, had just been born in Bethlehem. They would find the child lying in a manger, swaddled in cloth bands. Then, something even more spectacular happened—a mighty host of angels appeared, praising God! —Luke 2:8-14.

¹⁵ No wonder these humble men came rushing into Bethlehem! They must have been thrilled to see a newborn infant lying there just as the angel had described. They did not keep this good news to themselves. "They made known the saying . . . And all that heard marveled over the things told them by the shepherds." (Luke 2:17, 18) The religious leaders of the day evidently looked down on shepherds. But Jehovah clearly valued these humble, faithful men. How, though, did this visit affect Mary?

> Jehovah clearly valued the humble, faithful shepherds

¹⁶ Mary was surely exhausted from the rigors of childbirth, yet she listened intently to every word. And she did more: "Mary began to preserve all these sayings, drawing conclusions in her heart." (Luke 2:19) This young woman truly was thoughtful. She knew that this angelic message was vital. Her God, Jehovah, wanted her to know and to appreciate her son's identity and importance. So she did more than listen. She stored away the words in her heart so that she could ponder over them again and again in the months and years to come. Here is an outstanding key to the faith that Mary showed throughout her life.—*Read Hebrews 11:1.*

¹⁷ Will you follow Mary's example? Jehovah has filled the pages of his Word with vital spiritual truths. However, those truths can do us little good unless we first pay attention to them. We do that by reading the Bible regularly—not merely as a work of literature but as the inspired Word of God. (2 Tim. 3:16) Then, like Mary, we need to store up spiritual sayings in our heart, drawing conclusions. If we meditate on what we read in the Bible, contemplating ways that we can apply Jehovah's counsel more fully, we will give our faith the nourishment it needs to grow.

---

16. How did Mary show that she truly was thoughtful, revealing what key to her faith?

17. How can we follow Mary's example when it comes to spiritual truths?

Mary listened carefully to the shepherds and preserved their words in her heart

More Sayings to Preserve

18 On the baby's eighth day, Mary and Joseph had him circumcised as the Mosaic Law required, naming him Jesus, as directed. (Luke 1:31) Then, on the 40th day, they took him from Bethlehem to the temple in Jerusalem, some six miles away, and presented the purification offerings that the Law allowed for poorer folk—two turtledoves or two pigeons. If they felt shame in offering less than the ram and a turtledove that other parents could afford, they put such feelings aside. At any rate, they received powerful encouragement while they were there.—Luke 2:21-24.

19 An aged man named Simeon approached them and gave Mary even more sayings to treasure in her heart. He had been promised that he would see the Messiah before he died, and Jehovah's holy spirit indicated to him that little Jesus was the foretold Savior. Simeon also warned Mary of the pain that she would one day have to endure. He said that she would feel as if a long sword were run through her. (Luke 2:25-35) Even those forebod-

---

18. (a) How did Mary and Joseph obey the Mosaic Law in Jesus' early days? (b) What did the offering that Joseph and Mary gave at the temple reveal about their financial situation?

19. (a) How did Simeon give Mary more sayings to treasure in her heart? (b) What was Anna's reaction on seeing Jesus?

Mary and Joseph found rich encouragement at Jehovah's temple in Jerusalem

ing words may have helped Mary to endure when that hard time arrived, three decades later. After Simeon, a prophetess named Anna saw little Jesus and began speaking about him to everyone who cherished the hope of Jerusalem's deliverance.—*Read Luke 2:36-38.*

20 What a good decision Joseph and Mary had made in bringing their baby to Jehovah's temple in Jerusalem! They thus launched their son on a lifelong course of faithful attendance at Jehovah's temple. While there, they gave of themselves according to their ability and received words of instruction and encouragement. Mary surely left the temple that day stronger in faith, her heart full of spiritual sayings to meditate on and share with others.

21 It is a beautiful thing to see parents today following that example. Among Jehovah's Witnesses, parents faithfully bring their children to Christian meetings. Such parents give what they can, offering words of encouragement to their fellow believers. And they come away stronger, happier, and full of good things to share with others. What a pleasure it is to meet with them! As we do, we will find that our faith, like Mary's, will grow ever stronger.

---

20. How did bringing Jesus to the temple in Jerusalem prove to be a good decision?

21. How can we ensure that our faith will grow ever stronger, as Mary's did?

TO THINK ABOUT . . .

- How did Mary set an example in submissiveness and obedience?

- What can we learn from the way that Mary coped with poverty?

- How did Mary prove to be a thoughtful, spiritual woman?

- In what ways are you determined to follow Mary's example?

CHAPTER NINETEEN

He Protected, He Provided, He Persevered

JOSEPH swung another load onto the donkey's back. Picture him looking around at the darkened village of Bethlehem and patting the flank of the sturdy beast of burden. He was surely thinking of the long trip ahead. Egypt! A foreign people, a foreign tongue, foreign customs—how would his little family adapt to so much change?

2 It was not easy to tell the bad news to his beloved wife, Mary, but Joseph braced himself and did it. He told her of the dream in which an angel delivered this message from God: The king, Herod, wanted their little son dead! They had to leave right away. (**Read Matthew 2:13, 14.**) Mary was deeply concerned. How could anyone want to kill her innocent, harmless child? Neither Mary nor Joseph could fathom it. But they trusted in Jehovah, so they readied themselves.

3 Unaware of the unfolding drama, Bethlehem slept as Joseph, Mary, and Jesus slipped out of the village in the darkness. Heading southward, with the sky beginning to lighten in the east, Joseph likely wondered what lay ahead. How could a lowly carpenter protect his family against forces so powerful? Would he always be able to provide for his own? Would he manage to persevere in carrying out this heavy assignment that Jehovah God had given him, to care for and raise this unique child? Joseph faced daunting challenges. As we consider how he rose to meet each one, we will see why fathers today—and all of us—need to imitate the faith of Joseph.

Joseph Protected His Family

4 Months earlier, in his hometown of Nazareth, Joseph found

1, 2. (a) What changes did Joseph and his family face? (b) What bad news did Joseph have to tell his wife?

3. Describe the departure of Joseph and his family from Bethlehem. (See also the picture.)

4, 5. (a) How did Joseph's life change forever? (b) How did an angel encourage Joseph to take on a weighty assignment?

Joseph acted decisively and selflessly to protect his child

that his life changed forever after his engagement to the daughter of Heli. Joseph knew Mary as an innocent, faithful young woman. But then he learned that she was pregnant! He intended to divorce her secretly to protect her from scandal.* However, an angel spoke to him in a dream, explaining that Mary was pregnant by means of Jehovah's holy spirit. The angel added that the son she bore would "save his people from their sins." He further reassured Joseph: "Do not be afraid to take Mary your wife home."—Matt. 1:18-21.

⁵ Joseph, a righteous and obedient man, did just that. He took on the weightiest of assignments: raising and caring for a son who was not his own but who was most precious to God. Later, in obedience to an imperial decree, Joseph and his pregnant wife went to Bethlehem to register. It was there that the child was born.

⁶ Joseph did not take the family back to Nazareth. Instead, they settled in Bethlehem, just a few miles from Jerusalem. They were poor, but Joseph did all he could to protect Mary and Jesus from want or suffering. In a short time, they took up living in a humble home. Then, when Jesus was no longer a baby but a small child—perhaps over a year old—their lives suddenly changed again.

⁷ A group of men arrived, astrologers from the East, likely from faraway Babylon. They had followed a "star" to the home of Joseph and Mary and were looking for a child who was to become king of the Jews. The men were deeply respectful.

⁸ Whether they knew it or not, the astrologers had put little Jesus in great peril. The "star" they had seen led them first, not to Bethlehem, but to Jerusalem.# There they told wicked King Herod that they were looking for a child who was to become king of the Jews. Their report filled the man with jealous rage.

⁹ Happily, though, there were forces greater than Herod or Satan at work. How so? Well, when the visitors reached Jesus'

---

* In those days, engagement was viewed in almost the same light as marriage.
\# This "star" was no natural astronomical phenomenon; nor was it sent by God. Clearly, Satan used that supernatural manifestation as part of his wicked design to destroy Jesus.

6-8. (a) What events led to another change in the lives of Joseph and his little family? (b) What evidence suggests that Satan sent the "star"? (See also footnote.)

9-11. (a) In what ways were forces greater than Herod or Satan at work? (b) How did the journey to Egypt differ from what is described in apocryphal myths?

house and saw him with his mother, they brought out gifts, asking for nothing in return. How strange it must have been for Joseph and Mary to find themselves suddenly in possession of "gold and frankincense and myrrh"—valuable commodities! The astrologers intended to go back and tell King Herod just where they had found the child. However, Jehovah intervened. By means of a dream, he instructed the astrologers to return home by another route.—*Read Matthew 2:1-12.*

¹⁰ Shortly after the astrologers left, Joseph received this warning from Jehovah's angel: "Get up, take the young child and its mother and flee into Egypt, and stay there until I give you word; for Herod is about to search for the young child to destroy it." (Matt. 2:13) So, as we noted at the outset, Joseph obeyed swiftly. He

> ## Joseph sacrificed his own comfort for the sake of his family

put his child's safety above all else and took his family to Egypt. Because those pagan astrologers had brought such costly gifts, Joseph now had assets that might help the family during their sojourn ahead.

¹¹ Apocryphal myths and legends later romanticized the journey to Egypt, claiming that little Jesus miraculously shortened the trip, rendered bandits harmless, and even made date palms bend down to his mother to yield their fruit.* In truth, it was simply a long, arduous trek into the unknown.

¹² Parents can learn a lot from Joseph. He readily set aside his work and sacrificed his own comfort in order to protect his family from danger. Clearly, he viewed his family as a sacred trust from Jehovah. Parents today raise their children in a perilous world, a world full of forces that would endanger, corrupt, or even destroy young ones. How admirable it is when mothers and fathers act decisively, as Joseph did, working hard to protect their children from such influences!

Joseph Provided for His Family

¹³ It seems that the family did not stay long in Egypt, for soon the angel informed Joseph that Herod was dead. Joseph

---

* The Bible clearly shows that Jesus' first miracle, "the beginning of his signs," did not occur until after his baptism.—John 2:1-11.

12. Parents who are raising children in this perilous world can learn what from Joseph?

13, 14. How did Joseph and Mary end up raising their family in Nazareth?

Joseph trained
his son to become
a carpenter

brought his family back to their homeland. An ancient prophecy had foretold that Jehovah would call his Son "out of Egypt." (Matt. 2:15) Joseph helped to fulfill that prophecy, but where would he lead his family now?

14 Joseph was cautious. He wisely feared Herod's successor, Archelaus, who was likewise vicious and murderous. Divine guidance led Joseph to take his family up north, away from Jerusalem and all its intrigues, back to his hometown of Nazareth in Galilee. There he and Mary raised their family.—*Read Matthew 2: 19-23.*

15 They led a simple life—but not an easy one. The Bible refers to Joseph as the carpenter, using a word that embraces many ways of working with wood, such as cutting down timber, hauling it, and seasoning it for use in building houses, boats, small bridges, carts, wheels, yokes, and all kinds of farm implements. (Matt. 13:55) It was hard physical work. A carpenter in Bible times often worked near the doorway of his modest house or in a shop adjacent to it.

16 Joseph used a wide range of tools, some likely handed down from his father. He may have used a square, a plummet, a chalk line, a hatchet, a saw, an adze, a hammer, a mallet, chisels, a drill that he worked by pulling a bow back and forth, various glues, and perhaps some nails, though they were costly.

17 Imagine Jesus as a small boy watching his adoptive father at work. His eyes wide and intent on Joseph's every movement, he no doubt admired the strength in those broad shoulders and sinewy arms, the skill of the hands, the intelligence in the eyes. Perhaps Joseph began showing his young son how to perform such simple tasks as using dried fish skin to smooth out rough spots on wood. He likely taught Jesus the differences between the varieties of wood that he used—the sycamore fig, oak, or olive, for example.

15, 16. What was Joseph's work like, and what tools might he have used?

17, 18. (a) What did Jesus learn from his adoptive father? (b) Why did Joseph have to work ever harder at his trade?

¹⁸ Jesus learned, too, that those strong hands that felled trees, hewed beams, and pounded joints together were also gentle hands that caressed and comforted him, his mother, and his siblings. Yes, Joseph and Mary had a growing family that eventually included at least six children in addition to Jesus. (Matt. 13: 55, 56) Joseph had to work ever harder to care for and feed them all.

¹⁹ Joseph, however, understood that caring for his family's spiritual needs was paramount. So he spent time teaching his children about Jehovah God and His laws. He and Mary regularly took them to the local synagogue, where the Law was read aloud and explained. Perhaps Jesus was full of questions afterward, and Joseph tried hard to satisfy the boy's spiritual hunger. Joseph also took his family to religious festivals in Jerusalem. For the annual Passover, Joseph may have needed two weeks to make the 75-mile journey, observe the occasion, and return home.

> Joseph understood that caring for his family's spiritual needs was paramount

²⁰ Christian family heads today follow a similar pattern. They give of themselves for their children, putting spiritual training above every other concern, including material comforts. They go to great lengths to conduct family worship at home and to take their children to Christian meetings both large and small. Like Joseph, they know that there is no better investment they can make for the sake of their children.

"In Mental Distress"

²¹ When Jesus was 12 years old, Joseph took the family to Jerusalem as usual. It was Passover, a festive time, and large families traveled together in long caravans through the lush spring countryside. As they approached the starker landscapes near lofty Jerusalem, many would sing the familiar psalms of ascent. (Ps. 120-134) The city likely teemed with hundreds of thousands of people. Afterward, the families and their caravans began to head homeward. Joseph and Mary, perhaps with much to do, assumed that Jesus was traveling with others, maybe family members.

---

19. How did Joseph care for his family's spiritual needs?

20. How can Christian family heads follow the pattern set by Joseph?

21. What was Passover time like for Joseph's family, and when did Joseph and Mary notice that Jesus was missing?

Joseph regularly took his family to worship at the temple in Jerusalem

Only after Jerusalem lay a full day behind them did they realize a terrifying truth—Jesus was missing!—Luke 2:41-44.

²² Frantically, they retraced their steps all the way to Jerusalem. Imagine how empty and strange the city seemed to them now as they paced the streets, calling out their son's name. Where could the boy be? By the third day of searching, did Joseph begin to wonder if he had failed terribly in this sacred trust from Jehovah? Finally, they went to the temple. There they searched until they came upon a chamber where many learned men, versed in the Law, were gathered—with young Jesus sitting

22, 23. What did Joseph and Mary do about their missing boy and what did Mary say when they finally found him?

among them! Imagine the relief Joseph and Mary felt!—Luke 2: 45, 46.

23 Jesus was listening to the learned men and eagerly asking questions. The men were amazed at the child's understanding and his answers. Mary and Joseph, though, were astounded. In the Bible record, Joseph is silent. But Mary's words speak eloquently for both of them: "Child, why did you treat us this way? Here your father and I in mental distress have been looking for you."—Luke 2:47, 48.

24 Thus in a few deft strokes, God's Word paints a realistic picture of parenthood. It can be stressful—even when the child

24. How does the Bible paint a realistic picture of parenthood?

When Did Joseph Die?

We know that Joseph was alive when Jesus was 12 years old. At that age many Jewish youths began to learn their father's trade and became apprentices at 15. Joseph evidently lived long enough to teach Jesus to be a carpenter. Was Joseph still living when Jesus began his ministry at about 30 years of age? That seems very doubtful. Jesus' mother, brothers, and sisters are all mentioned as living at that time but not Joseph. Jesus was once even called "the son of Mary," not the son of Joseph. (Mark 6:3) Mary is spoken of as acting and taking initiatives on her own, without consulting a husband. (John 2:1-5) That would have been unusual in Bible times unless she was a widow. Finally, as he was dying, Jesus entrusted the care of his mother to the apostle John. (John 19:26, 27) There would have been no need to do so if Joseph were still living. Likely, then, Joseph died when Jesus was still a relatively young man. As the eldest son, Jesus undoubtedly took over the carpentry business and cared for the family until his baptism.

is perfect! Parenting in today's dangerous world can bring untold "mental distress," but fathers and mothers can take comfort in knowing that the Bible acknowledges the challenge they face.

25 Jesus had stayed in the one place in the world where he felt the closest to his heavenly Father, Jehovah, eagerly soaking up anything he could learn. He answered his parents in simple sincerity: "Why did you have to go looking for me? Did you not know that I must be in the house of my Father?"—Luke 2:49.

26 Joseph surely thought about those words many times. Perhaps he came to beam with pride over them. After all, he had worked diligently to teach his adopted son to feel that way about Jehovah God. By that time in his life as a boy, Jesus already had warm feelings about the word "father"—feelings shaped largely by his years with Joseph.

27 If you are a father, do you realize how privileged you are to help your children to form a concept of what a loving, protective father is? Likewise, if you have stepchildren or adopted children, remember Joseph's example and treat each child as unique and precious. Help those children to draw closer to their heavenly Father, Jehovah God.—*Read Ephesians 6:4.*

Joseph Persevered Faithfully

28 The Bible discloses only a few more traces of Joseph's life, but they are worth considering carefully. We read that Jesus "continued subject to them"—his parents. We

25, 26. How did Jesus answer his parents, and how might Joseph have felt about his son's words?

27. As a father, how are you privileged, and why should you remember Joseph's example?

28, 29. (a) What do the words recorded at Luke 2:51, 52 reveal about Joseph? (b) Joseph played what role in helping his son progress in wisdom?

also find that "Jesus went on progressing in wisdom and in physical growth and in favor with God and men." (*Read Luke 2:51, 52.*) What do those words reveal about Joseph? Several things. We learn that Joseph continued taking the lead in his household, for his perfect son respected his father's authority and remained in subjection to it.

29 We further learn that Jesus continued to grow in wisdom. Joseph surely had much to do with his son's progress in that regard. In those days, there was a time-honored proverb among the Jews. It can still be found and read today. The saying asserts that only men of leisure can become truly wise, whereas tradesmen, such as carpenters, farmers, and blacksmiths, "cannot declare justice and judgment; and they shall not be found where parables are spoken." Later, Jesus exposed the emptiness of that proverb. As a boy, how often he had heard his adoptive father, humble carpenter though he was, teach effectively about Jehovah's "justice and judgment"! No doubt, there were countless occasions.

30 We can also see evidence of Joseph's influence in Jesus' physical growth. A well-cared-for boy, Jesus grew into a strong, healthy man. Further, Joseph trained his son to be skilled at his physical work. Jesus was known not only as the carpenter's son but also as "the carpenter." (Mark 6:3) So Joseph's training was successful. Family heads wisely imitate Joseph, caring for the practical well-being of their children and ensuring that they can support themselves.

31 Once we reach the point in the Bible record where Jesus is baptized at about the age of 30, we find that Joseph is no longer part of the story. Evidence suggests that Mary was a widow by the time Jesus began his ministry. (See the box "When Did Joseph Die?") Yet, Joseph left a clear mark —a shining example of a father who protected his family, provided for them, and persevered faithfully to the end. Any father, any family head, or any other Christian would do well to imitate the faith of Joseph.

30. How did Joseph set an example for family heads today?

31. (a) What does evidence suggest regarding the end of Joseph's life? (Include the box.) (b) What example did Joseph leave for us to imitate?

TO THINK ABOUT . . .

- In what ways did Joseph act to protect his family?

- How did Joseph provide for those who were his own?

- What shows that Joseph persevered in his God-given assignment?

- In what ways would you like to imitate the example of Joseph?

171

CHAPTER TWENTY

"I Have Believed"

MARTHA could see it in her mind's eye—her brother's tomb, a cave sealed with a stone against the entrance. Her grief was a burden as cold and heavy as that rock. She could barely believe that her beloved Lazarus was gone. The four days since he had taken his last breath seemed like one long blur of mourning, visitors, and condolences.

² And now, standing before Martha was the man who had meant the most to Lazarus. Seeing Jesus likely brought her grief into sharp focus, for he was the one person in all the world who could have saved her brother. Still, Martha found some comfort in being with Jesus here outside the little hillside town of Bethany. In her few moments with him, she again felt warmed by the kindness in his eyes, the keen empathy that was always so encouraging. He asked her questions that helped her to focus on her faith and on her beliefs about the resurrection. The conversation led Martha to make one of the most important statements that would ever pass her lips: "I have believed that you are the Christ the Son of God, the One coming into the world."—John 11:27.

³ As those words show, Martha was a woman of remarkable faith. What little the Bible tells us of her imparts profound lessons that can help us strengthen our own faith. To see how that is so, let us consider the first account about Martha in the Bible.

"Anxious and Disturbed"

⁴ It was months earlier. Lazarus was alive and well. His home in Bethany was about to receive the most important of visitors,

1. Describe Martha's grief and its cause.
2, 3. (a) Seeing Jesus likely had what effect on Martha? (b) What did Martha's important statement show about her?
4. In what way was Martha's family unusual, and what was the family's relationship with Jesus?

Jesus Christ. Lazarus, Martha, and Mary were an unusual family —three grown siblings who evidently shared a home. Some researchers suggest that Martha may have been the eldest of the three, since she seems to have acted as hostess and at times is mentioned first. (John 11:5) There is no way of knowing whether any of the three were ever married. At any rate, they became close friends of Jesus. During his ministry in Judea, where he met so much opposition and hostility, Jesus made their home his base. No doubt, he greatly appreciated that haven of peace and support.

⁵ Martha had much to do with the comfort and hospitality of the home. A busy, industrious soul, she often seems to have been in a flurry of activity. The present occasion of Jesus' visit was no exception. She soon planned a special meal with many dishes for her distinguished guest and, perhaps, some of his traveling companions. Back then, hospitality was very important. When a guest arrived, he was welcomed with a kiss, his sandals were removed, his feet were washed, and his head was greased with refreshing perfumed oil. (**Read Luke 7:44-47.**) As to his accommodations and nourishment, every care was to be taken.

⁶ Martha and Mary had their work cut out for them. Mary, who is sometimes thought of as the more sensitive and contemplative of the two, surely helped her sister out at first. But after Jesus arrived, things changed. He viewed the occasion as a time to teach—and teach he did! Unlike the religious leaders of the day, Jesus respected women and readily taught them about God's Kingdom, the theme of his ministry. Mary, thrilled at this opportunity, sat at his feet and took in every word.

⁷ We can just imagine the tension rising within Martha's heart. With all the dishes she had to prepare and all the duties she had to carry out for her guests, she became more and more anxious and distracted. As she passed to and fro on her busy way and saw her sister sitting there doing nothing to help her, did she color slightly, sigh audibly, or frown? It would not be surprising if she did. She could not do all this work on her own!

5, 6. (a) Why was Martha particularly busy during Jesus' present visit? (b) How did Mary respond to the opportunity afforded by Jesus' presence at their home?

7, 8. Why did tension rise within Martha's heart, and how did she finally express it?

8 Finally, Martha could no longer suppress her frustration. She interrupted Jesus, blurting out: "Lord, does it not matter to you that my sister has left me alone to attend to things? Tell her, therefore, to join in helping me." (Luke 10:40) These were strong words. A number of translations render her question to this effect: "Lord, do you not care . . . ?" Then she asked Jesus to correct Mary, to order her back to work.

9 Jesus' reply may have surprised Martha, as it has many Bible readers since. He gently said: "Martha, Martha, you are anxious and disturbed about many things. A few things, though, are needed, or just one. For her part, Mary chose the good portion, and it will not be taken away from her." (Luke 10:41, 42) What did Jesus mean? Was he calling Martha a materialist? Was he dismissing her hard work in preparing a fine meal?

10 No. Jesus clearly saw that Martha's motives were loving and pure. Further, he did not feel that even bounteous hospitality was necessarily wrong. He had willingly attended Matthew's "big reception feast" for him sometime earlier. (Luke 5:29) Martha's meal was not the key issue here; rather, it was her priorities. So focused was she on her elaborate meal that she lost sight of what mattered most. What was that?

11 Jesus, the only-begotten Son of Jehovah God, was in Martha's home to teach the truth. Nothing, including her lovely meal and preparations, could be more important. Jesus was no doubt saddened that Martha was missing out on a unique opportunity to deepen her faith, but he let her make her own choice.* It was quite another thing, though, for Martha to ask Jesus to coerce Mary into missing out as well.

> Jesus appreciated Martha's hospitality, and he knew that her motives were loving and pure

12 So he gently corrected Martha, repeating her name soothingly to calm her agitated nerves, and he assured her that there was no need to be "anxious and disturbed about many things." A simple meal of one or two dishes would be sufficient,

---

* In first-century Jewish society, women were generally excluded from academic activities. Their training tended to focus on duties in the home. Martha may thus have seen it as highly unusual for a woman to sit at the feet of a scholar to learn.

9, 10. (a) How did Jesus reply to Martha? (b) How do we know that Jesus was not dismissing Martha's hard work?

11, 12. How did Jesus gently correct Martha?

especially when a spiritual feast was available. By no means, then, would he take away from Mary "the good portion" she had chosen—that of learning from Jesus!

¹³ This little domestic scene is rich in lessons for Christ's followers today. We must never allow anything to crowd out the filling of our "spiritual need." (Matt. 5:3) While we want to imitate Martha's generous, industrious spirit, we never want to become so "anxious and disturbed" about the less essential part of hospitality that we miss out on what matters most. We associate with fellow believers, not primarily for the sake of serving or receiving sumptuous food, but mainly for an interchange

13. What lessons can we learn from the way that Jesus corrected Martha?

Though "anxious and disturbed about many things," Martha humbly accepted correction

of encouragement and the imparting of spiritual gifts. (**Read Romans 1:11, 12.**) Even the simplest meal may make such an upbuilding occasion possible.

A Beloved Brother Lost—And Restored

14 Did Martha accept Jesus' gentle reproof and learn from it? We need not wonder. The apostle John, in introducing a thrilling account about Martha's brother, reminds us: "Now Jesus loved Martha and her sister and Lazarus." (John 11:5) Months had passed since Jesus' visit to Bethany described above. Clearly, Martha had not indulged in sulking; she was not nursing a grudge against Jesus for his loving counsel. She had taken it to heart. In this matter too, she set an excellent example of faith for us, for who of us does not need a little correction at times?

15 When her brother took ill, Martha surely busied herself with his care. She did everything in her power to soothe his discomfort and help him get better. Nonetheless, Lazarus sank still deeper into his illness. Hour after hour, his sisters stayed by his side to care for him. How often Martha must have gazed into her brother's haggard face, remembering their many years together and the joys and sorrows they had shared!

16 When it looked as if Lazarus was beyond their help, Martha and Mary sent a message to Jesus. He was preaching some two days' journey away. Their message was simple: "Lord, see! the one for whom you have affection is sick." (John 11:1, 3) They knew that Jesus loved their brother, and they had faith that he would do whatever he could to help his friend. Did they cling to the hope that Jesus might arrive before it was too late? If so, their hopes were dashed. Lazarus died.

17 Together, Martha and Mary mourned their brother, taking care of the preparations for his burial and receiving the many guests from Bethany and its environs. Still, no news of Jesus. Martha may have grown more puzzled as the time passed. Finally, four days after Lazarus' death, Martha heard that Jesus was nearing the town. Ever the woman of action, even in this grim

14. Why can we be sure that Martha set a good example in accepting correction?

15, 16. (a) How did Martha surely respond when her brother took ill? (b) Why were Martha's and Mary's hopes dashed?

17. What puzzled Martha, and how did she react when she heard that Jesus was nearing the town?

Martha's faith in Jesus was rewarded when she and Mary saw their brother resurrected

hour, Martha got up and, without telling Mary, rushed out to meet Jesus.—*Read John 11:18-20.*

¹⁸ When Martha caught sight of her Master, she put into words the thought that had been tormenting her and Mary for days: "Lord, if you had been here my brother would not have died." But hope and faith were not dead in Martha. She added: "And yet at present I know that as many things as you ask God for, God will give you." Jesus immediately said something to strengthen her faith: "Your brother will rise."—John 11:21-23.

¹⁹ Martha thought that Jesus was talking about the future resurrection, so she replied: "I know he will rise in the resurrection on the last day." (John 11:24) Her faith in that teaching was remarkable. Some Jewish religious leaders, called Sadducees, denied that there would be a resurrection, though it was a clear

18, 19. Martha expressed what hope and why was her faith remarkable?

177

teaching in the inspired Scriptures. (Dan. 12:13; Mark 12:18) Martha knew, however, that Jesus taught the resurrection hope and had even performed resurrections—although not of anyone who had been dead as long as Lazarus had. She did not know what lay ahead.

20 Jesus then made an unforgettable statement: "I am the resurrection and the life." Indeed, Jehovah God has given his Son the authority to perform resurrections on a global scale in the future. Jesus asked Martha: "Do you believe this?" Then she gave the answer discussed at the outset of this chapter. She had faith that Jesus was the Christ, or Messiah, that he was the Son of Jehovah God, and that he was the one whom the prophets had foretold would come into the world.—John 5:28, 29; *read John 11:25-27.*

21 Do Jehovah God and his Son, Jesus Christ, value faith like that of Martha? The events that next unfolded before Martha's eyes provide the clearest of answers. She hurried to get her sister. Thereafter, she saw that Jesus was deeply moved as he talked to Mary and the many mourners with her. She saw the tears come to his eyes as he freely showed his deep grief over the pain that death causes. She heard Jesus order that the stone be rolled away from her brother's tomb.—John 11:28-39.

22 Ever practical, Martha objected that the body would smell by now, four days after death. Jesus reminded her: "Did I not tell you that if you would believe you would see the glory of God?" She did believe, and she did see the glory of Jehovah God. Right then and there, he empowered his Son to bring Lazarus back to life! Think of the moments that must have been etched in Martha's memory to the end of her days: Jesus' commanding call, "Lazarus, come on out!"; the faint noise from the cave where Lazarus was entombed as the man rose and, still bound in the bandages used to prepare the body, inched his way to the door of the cave; Jesus' command to "loose him and let him go"; and, to be sure, the ecstatic embrace as Martha and Mary flew into their brother's arms. (*Read John 11:40-44.*) The burden on Martha's heart was lifted!

---

20. Explain the meaning of Jesus' unforgettable statement recorded at John 11:25-27 and of Martha's reply.

21, 22. (a) How did Jesus reveal his feelings for those who mourn? (b) Describe the resurrection of Lazarus.

23 This account shows that the resurrection of the dead is not mere wishful thinking; it is a heartwarming Bible teaching and a proven historical reality. (Job 14:14, 15) Jehovah and his Son love to reward faith, as they did in the case of Martha, Mary, and Lazarus. They have such rewards in store for you too if you build strong faith.

"Martha Was Ministering"

24 The Bible record mentions Martha just one more time. It was at the outset of the final week of Jesus' life on earth. Knowing well what hardships lay ahead of him, Jesus again chose that haven at Bethany as his residence. From there he would walk the two miles to Jerusalem. Jesus and Lazarus were dining at the home of Simon the leper, and there we get this last glimpse of our subject: "Martha was ministering."—John 12:2.

25 How typical of that industrious woman! When we first come upon her in the Bible, she is working; when we leave her, she is still working, doing her best to care for the needs of those around her. Congregations of Christ's followers today are blessed to have women like Martha—stouthearted and generous, always putting their faith into action by giving of themselves. Did Martha keep doing just that? It seems likely. If so, she acted wisely, for she had yet to meet her share of obstacles.

26 Within days, Martha had to endure the terrible death of her beloved Master, Jesus. Further, the same murderous hypocrites who killed him were determined to kill Lazarus as well, since his resurrection was boosting the faith of so many. (*Read John 12:9-11.*) And, of course, death did eventually sever the loving bonds that joined Martha to her siblings. We do not know how or when that happened, but we may be fairly sure of this: Martha's precious faith helped her endure to the end. That is why Christians today do well to imitate the faith of Martha.

23. What do Jehovah and Jesus want to do for you, and what do you need to do?

24. The Bible record gives us what last glimpse of Martha?

25. Why are congregations today blessed to have women like Martha?

26. What did Martha's faith help her to do?

TO THINK ABOUT . . .
- What can we learn from the counsel Jesus gave Martha?
- In what ways did Martha display a giving, industrious spirit?
- How did Martha show remarkable faith?
- In what ways would you like to imitate the faith of Martha?

CHAPTER TWENTY-ONE

He Fought Against Fear and Doubt

PETER strained against the oar and peered into the night. Was that a faint glow he saw on the eastern horizon, a sign of dawn at last? The muscles of his back and shoulders burned from long hours of rowing. The wind that whipped his hair about had churned the Sea of Galilee into a rage. Wave after wave crashed against the prow of the fishing boat, soaking him with cold spray. He rowed on.

2 Somewhere back there on shore, Peter and his companions had left Jesus by himself. That day, they had seen Jesus feed a hungry crowd of thousands with just a few loaves and fish. The people responded by seeking to make Jesus king, but he wanted no part of politics. He was also determined to keep his followers from cultivating such ambitions. Evading the crowds, he compelled his disciples to board the boat and head for the opposite shore while he went up into the mountain alone to pray. —Mark 6:35-45; *read John 6:14-17.*

> In two years, Peter had learned a great deal from Jesus, but he still had much to learn

3 The moon, nearly full, had been high overhead when the disciples set out; now it was sinking slowly toward the western horizon. Yet, they had managed to travel only a few miles. The exertion and the constant roar of the wind and the waves made conversation difficult. Likely, Peter was alone with his thoughts.

4 How much there was to think about! Peter had first met Jesus of Nazareth over two eventful years earlier. He had learned

---

1-3. What had Peter witnessed during an eventful day, and what kind of night was he experiencing?

4. What struggles make Peter's example an outstanding one for us to imitate?

a great deal, but he still had much to learn. His willingness to do so—to struggle against such obstacles as doubt and fear—make him an outstanding example for us to imitate. Let us see why.

"We Have Found the Messiah"!

5 Peter would never forget the day he met Jesus. His brother, Andrew, had first brought him the astounding news: "We have found the Messiah." With those words, Peter's life began to change. It would never again be the same.—John 1:41.

6 Peter lived in Capernaum, a city on the northern shore of a freshwater lake called the Sea of Galilee. He and Andrew were partners with James and John, the sons of Zebedee, in a fishing business. Living with Peter were not only his wife but also his mother-in-law and his brother, Andrew. To support such a household by fishing surely required hard work, energy, and resourcefulness. We can imagine the countless long nights of labor—the men letting out the dragnets between two boats and hauling aboard whatever catch the lake afforded. We can also picture toilsome daylight hours as the fish were sorted and sold, the nets mended and cleaned.

7 Andrew, the Bible tells us, was a disciple of John the Baptist. Peter surely listened to his brother's reports about John's message with intense interest. One day, Andrew saw John point out Jesus of Nazareth and say: "See, the Lamb of God!" Andrew immediately became a follower of Jesus and eagerly told Peter this thrilling news: The Messiah had arrived! (John 1:35-40) After the rebellion in Eden some 4,000 years earlier, Jehovah God had promised that a special individual would come to provide real hope for mankind. (Gen. 3:15) Andrew had met this very Rescuer, the Messiah himself! Peter hurried off to meet Jesus as well.

8 Until that day, Peter was known by the name Simon, or Simeon. But Jesus looked at him and said: " 'You are Simon the son of John; you will be called Cephas' (which is translated Peter)." (John 1:42) "Cephas" is a common noun meaning "stone," or "rock." Evidently, Jesus' words were prophetic. He foresaw that Peter would become like a rock—a stable, sturdy, and reliable influence among Christ's followers. Did Peter see himself

---

5, 6. What kind of life did Peter lead?

7. What did Peter come to hear about Jesus, and why was the news thrilling?

8. What was the meaning of the name Jesus bestowed on Peter, and why do some still question that choice of a name?

that way? It seems doubtful. Even some modern-day readers of the Gospel accounts see little that is rocklike in Peter. Some have suggested that his character as revealed in the Bible record seems to be unsteady, inconstant, vacillating.

9 Peter did have his faults. Jesus was not blind to those. But Jesus, like his Father, Jehovah, was always looking for the good in people. Jesus saw much potential in Peter, and He sought to help him build on those good qualities. Jehovah and his Son look for the good in us today too. We may have a hard time believing that there is much good in us for them to find. However, we need to trust their viewpoint and prove ourselves willing to be trained and molded, as Peter was.—*Read 1 John 3:19, 20.*

"Stop Being Afraid"

10 Peter likely accompanied Jesus on part of the preaching tour that ensued. He may thus have seen Jesus perform his first miracle, that of turning water into wine at the wedding feast in Cana. More important, he heard Jesus' marvelous and hope-filled message about the Kingdom of God. Still, he tore himself away and returned to his fishing business. Some months later, though, Peter was again face-to-face with Jesus—and this time Jesus invited Peter to follow him full-time as a way of life.

11 Peter had just endured a discouraging night's work. Again and again, the fishermen had let down their nets, only to haul them in empty. Peter surely brought all his experience and ingenuity to bear on the problem, trying various spots in the lake to find where the fish were feeding. No doubt, there were times when he, like so many fishermen, wished he could peer right into the murky waters to find the schools of fish or somehow will them into his nets. Of course, such thoughts could only deepen his frustration. This was no pleasure sport for Peter; people depended on him to catch fish. Finally, he came ashore empty-handed. The nets had to be cleaned. He was thus busily engaged when Jesus approached.

12 A crowd was pressing in on Jesus, eagerly taking in his every word. Hemmed in by them, Jesus got into Peter's boat and asked him to pull away a bit from land. With his voice carrying

---

9. What do Jehovah and his Son look for, and why, do you think, should we trust their point of view?

10. What did Peter likely witness, yet to what did he return?

11, 12. (a) What kind of night's work had Peter endured? (b) Listening to Jesus likely brought what questions to Peter's mind?

clearly over the water, Jesus taught the crowd. Peter listened with rapt attention, as did those ashore. He never tired of hearing Jesus develop the central theme of his preaching—the Kingdom of God. What a privilege it would be to help the Christ spread this message of hope throughout the land! But would that be practical? How would Peter feed his family? Perhaps Peter thought again of the long and fruitless night behind him.—Luke 5:1-3.

13 When Jesus finished speaking, he told Peter: "Pull out to where it is deep, and you men let down your nets for a catch." Peter was full of doubt. He said: "Instructor, for a whole night we toiled and took nothing, but at your bidding I will lower the nets." Peter had just washed off the nets. Surely the last thing he wanted to do was lower them yet again—especially now when the fish would not even be feeding! Still, he complied, likely signaling to his partners in a second boat to follow them. —Luke 5:4, 5.

14 Peter felt an unexpected weight as he started hauling in the nets. Incredulous, he pulled harder, and before long he could see a great mass of fish wriggling within the mesh! Frantically, he motioned to the men in the second boat to come to help. As they did, it soon became apparent that one boat could not contain all these fish. They filled both vessels, but there were too many—the boats started to sink under the weight. Peter was overwhelmed with astonishment. He had seen Christ's power in action before, but this instance was so personal. Here was a man who could even cause the fish to enter the nets! Fear welled up in Peter. He sank to his knees and said: "Depart from me, because I am a sinful man, Lord." How could he ever prove worthy to associate with One who wielded the very power of God in such ways?—*Read Luke 5:6-9.*

15 Jesus kindly said: "Stop being afraid. From now on you will be catching men alive." (Luke 5:10, 11) This was no time for doubt or fear. Peter's doubts about such practical matters as fishing were unfounded; his fears about his own faults and

Peter never tired of hearing Jesus develop the central theme of his preaching —the Kingdom of God

13, 14. What miracle did Jesus perform for Peter, and how did Peter react?
15. How did Jesus teach Peter that his doubts and fears were unfounded?

inadequacies were just as baseless. Jesus had a great work to do, a ministry that would change history. He served a God who "will forgive in a large way." (Isa. 55:7) Jehovah would take care of Peter's needs, both physical and spiritual.—Matt. 6:33.

16 Peter responded quickly, as did James and John. "They brought the boats back to land, and abandoned everything and followed him." (Luke 5:11) Peter put faith in Jesus and in the One who sent him. It was the best decision he could make. Christians today who overcome their doubt and fear to take up service to God are likewise showing faith. Such trust in Jehovah is never misplaced.—Ps. 22:4, 5.

16. How did Peter, James, and John respond to Jesus' invitation, and why was it the best decision they could make?

"I am a sinful man, Lord"

"Why Did You Give Way to Doubt?"

[17] Some two years after meeting Jesus, Peter rowed through that windy night on the Sea of Galilee, as mentioned at the outset of this chapter. Of course, we cannot know what memories crossed his mind. There were so many to choose from! Jesus had healed Peter's mother-in-law. He had delivered the Sermon on the Mount. Again and again, through his teaching and his powerful works, he had demonstrated that he was Jehovah's Chosen One, the Messiah. As the months passed, Peter's faults, such as his tendency to give in to impulses of fear and doubt, had surely subsided to a degree. Jesus had even chosen Peter to be one of the 12 apostles! Still, Peter had not yet vanquished fear and doubt, as he would soon learn.

[18] During the fourth watch of that night, or sometime between 3:00 a.m. and sunrise, Peter suddenly stopped rowing and sat bolt upright. There—across the waves—something was moving! Was it the spray of the waves catching the moonlight? No, it was too steady, too upright. It was a man! Yes, a man, and he was walking on the surface of the sea! As the figure neared, it looked as though he was going to walk right by them. Terrified, the disciples thought it was some kind of apparition. The man spoke: "Take courage, it is I; have no fear." It was Jesus!—Matt. 14:25-28.

[19] Peter responded: "Lord, if it is you, command me to come to you over the waters." His first impulse was a courageous one. Full of excitement at this unique miracle, Peter sought to have his faith further confirmed. He wanted to be part of the action. Kindly, Jesus beckoned him. Peter clambered over the side of the vessel and down onto the undulating surface of the sea. Imagine Peter's sensation as he found solid footing beneath him and then stood on top of the waters. He must have been filled with wonder as he made his way toward Jesus. However, another impulse soon welled up in him.—*Read Matthew 14:29.*

[20] Peter needed to keep his focus on Jesus. It was Jesus, using the power of Jehovah, who was keeping Peter above the

---

17. Peter had what memories of the two years since meeting Jesus?

18, 19. (a) Describe what Peter saw on the Sea of Galilee. (b) How did Jesus grant Peter's request?

20. (a) How did Peter lose his focus, and with what result? (b) What lesson did Jesus drive home to Peter?

wind-swept waves. And Jesus was doing so in response to Peter's faith in him. But Peter got distracted. We read: "Looking at the windstorm, he got afraid." Peter took in an eyeful of those waves crashing against the boat, tossing spray and foam to the wind, and he panicked. He probably imagined himself sinking in that lake, drowning there. As fear rose in his heart, his faith sank. The man who had been named Rock because of his potential for steadiness began to sink like a stone because of his wavering faith. Peter was an able swimmer, but he did not rely on that ability now. He cried out: "Lord, save me!" Jesus caught him by the hand and pulled him up. Then, while still on the water's surface, he drove home this important lesson to Peter: "You with little faith, why did you give way to doubt?"—Matt. 14: 30, 31.

[21] "Give way to doubt"—what an apt phrase! Doubt can be a powerful, destructive force. If we yield to it, it can eat away at our faith and cause us to sink spiritually. We need to fight back vigorously! How? By keeping the right focus. If we dwell on what scares us, what discourages us, what distracts us from Jehovah and his Son, we will find our doubts growing. If we focus on Jehovah and his Son, on what they have done, are doing, and will do for those who love them, we will keep corrosive doubts at bay.

[22] As Peter followed Jesus up into the boat, he saw the storm die down. Quiet fell on the Sea of Galilee. Peter joined his fellow disciples in declaring: "You are really God's Son." (Matt. 14:33) As dawn broke over the lake, Peter's heart must have soared. He repudiated doubt and fear. Granted, he had a long way to go before he became the rocklike Christian that Jesus foresaw. But he was determined to keep trying, to keep growing. Do you have such determination? You will find that Peter's faith is worth imitating.

TO THINK ABOUT . . .

- How did Peter overcome his doubts about following Jesus?
- How did Jesus show that he saw the good in Peter?
- On the Sea of Galilee, what did Peter learn about giving way to doubt?
- In what ways would you like to imitate Peter's faith?

---

21. Why is doubt dangerous, and how can we fight against it?

22. Why is Peter's faith worth imitating?

"Looking at the windstorm, he got afraid"

CHAPTER TWENTY-TWO

He Was Loyal in the Face of Tests

PETER gazed anxiously around at the faces of Jesus' audience. The setting was the synagogue in Capernaum. Peter's home was in this town; his fishing business was here, on the northern shore of the Sea of Galilee; many of his friends, relatives, and business acquaintances lived here. No doubt Peter was hoping that his townsmen would see Jesus as he did and that they would share the thrill of learning about God's Kingdom from the greatest of all teachers. No such outcome seemed likely that day.

² Many had stopped listening. Some were murmuring audibly, objecting to the thrust of Jesus' message. Most troubling to Peter, though, was the reaction of some of Jesus' own disciples. Their faces no longer bore that happy expression of enlightenment, the thrill of discovery, the joy of learning the truth. Now, they looked upset, even bitter. Some spoke up, calling Jesus' speech shocking. Refusing to listen anymore, they left the synagogue—and quit following Jesus as well.—*Read John 6:60, 66.*

³ It was a difficult time for Peter and for his fellow apostles. Peter did not fully grasp what Jesus said that day. No doubt he could see why Jesus' words might seem offensive if taken at face value. What would Peter do? It was not the first time that his loyalty to his Master was tested; nor would it be the last. Let us see how Peter's faith helped him to rise to such challenges and remain loyal.

Loyal When Others Turned Disloyal

⁴ Peter often found himself surprised by Jesus. Again and again, his Master acted and spoke in a way that was contrary to

1, 2. What was Peter likely hoping for as Jesus spoke in Capernaum, yet what happened instead?

3. What did Peter's faith help him to do a number of times?

4, 5. How had Jesus acted in ways that were contrary to what people expected of him?

what people expected of Him. Just a day earlier, Jesus had miraculously fed a crowd of thousands. In response, they had attempted to make him king. Yet, he surprised many by withdraw-
ing from them, directing his disciples to board a boat and sail
toward Capernaum. As the disciples made their way over water
during the night, Jesus surprised them again by walking across
the stormy Sea of Galilee, giving Peter an important lesson in
faith.

5 In the morning, they soon found that those crowds had
followed them around the lake. Evidently, though, the people
were driven by a desire to see Jesus produce more food miraculously, not by any hunger for spiritual truths. Jesus rebuked
them for their materialistic spirit. (John 6:25-27) That discussion
continued at the synagogue in Capernaum, where Jesus again
went against expectations in an effort to teach a vital but difficult truth.

6 Jesus wanted those people to see him, not as a source of
mere physical food, but as a spiritual provision from God, as the
one whose life and death as a man would make eternal life possible for others. So he gave an illustration comparing himself to
manna, the bread that came down from heaven in Moses' day.
When some objected, he used a vivid illustration, explaining
that it was necessary to partake of his flesh and his blood in order to attain life. It was at this point that the objections became
insistent. Some said: "This speech is shocking; who can listen to
it?" Many of Jesus' own disciples decided to quit following him.*
—John 6:48-60, 66.

7 What would Peter do? He too must have been baffled by
Jesus' speech. He did not yet grasp that Jesus must die in order
to carry out God's will. Was Peter tempted to slink off like those
fickle disciples who left Jesus that day? No; something important set Peter apart from those men. What was it?

8 Jesus turned to his apostles and said: "You do not want to
go also, do you?" (John 6:67) He addressed the 12, but it was
Peter who spoke up. It was often so. Peter may have been the

---

* We can see the inconstancy of the crowd at the synagogue if we compare their
reactions to Jesus' speech here with their expressions just the day before when they
enthusiastically proclaimed him a prophet of God.—John 6:14.

---

6. What illustration did Jesus give, and how did his listeners react?

7, 8. (a) What did Peter not yet grasp about Jesus' role? (b) How did Peter answer Jesus' question to the apostles?

oldest of them. In any case, he was certainly the most outspoken of the group; rarely, it seems, did Peter hesitate to say what was on his mind. In this case, what was on his mind was this beautiful and memorable statement: "Lord, whom shall we go away to? You have sayings of everlasting life."—John 6:68.

⁹ Do not those words touch your heart? Peter's faith in Jesus had helped him to build a priceless quality—loyalty. Peter saw clearly that Jesus was the only Savior Jehovah had provided and that Jesus saved by means of his sayings—his teachings about the Kingdom of God. Peter knew that even if there were some things that puzzled him, there was nowhere else to go if he wanted God's favor and the blessing of everlasting life.

¹⁰ Is that how you feel? Sadly, many in today's world claim to love Jesus but fail the test of loyalty. Genuine loyalty to Christ requires that we share Peter's view of Jesus' teachings. We need to learn them, to grasp their meaning, and to live by them—even when they surprise us by running contrary to our expectations or personal preferences. Only by proving loyal can we hope to attain to the everlasting life that Jesus wants for us.—*Read Psalm 97:10.*

Loyal When Corrected

¹¹ Not long after that busy time, Jesus led his apostles and some disciples on a long trek northward. The snowcapped peak of Mount Hermon, at the northernmost limit of the Promised Land, was at times visible even from the blue waters of the Sea of Galilee. Gradually, that mountain loomed higher as the group approached, following the rising terrain up to the villages near Caesarea Philippi.* In this lovely setting, with a perspective over much of the Promised Land to the south, Jesus asked his followers an important question.

¹² "Who are the crowds saying that I am?" he wanted to know. We can just imagine Peter looking into Jesus' keen eyes,

---

* From the shores of the Sea of Galilee, that 30-mile journey took the group from about 700 feet below sea level to 1,150 feet above, through regions of great natural beauty.

---

9. How did Peter show loyalty to Jesus?

10. How can we today imitate Peter's loyalty?

11. Jesus led his followers on what trek? (See also footnote.)

12, 13. (a) Why did Jesus ask about the crowds and their view of him? (b) In his words to Jesus, how did Peter show genuine faith?

sensing again his Master's kindness and his powerful, clear intelligence. Jesus was interested in the conclusions his audiences were drawing from what they saw and heard. Jesus' disciples answered the question, repeating some of the popular misconceptions surrounding Jesus' identity. But Jesus wanted to know more. Were his closest followers making the same mistakes? "You, though, who do you say I am?" he asked.—Luke 9:18-20.

13 Again, Peter was quick to respond. He put into clear, bold words the conclusion that had formed in the hearts of many there. "You are the Christ, the Son of the living God," he said. We can imagine Jesus giving Peter a smile of approval as He commended him warmly. Jesus reminded Peter that it was Jehovah God—not any man—who had made this vital truth so plain to those with genuine faith. Peter had been enabled to discern one of the greatest truths Jehovah had yet revealed—the identity of the long-promised Messiah, or Christ!—*Read Matthew 16: 16, 17.*

> We need to be loyal to Jesus' teachings, even when they run contrary to our expectations or personal preference

14 This Christ was the one called in ancient prophecy a stone that the builders would reject. (Ps. 118:22; Luke 20:17) With such prophecies in mind, Jesus revealed that Jehovah would establish a congregation on the very stone, or rock-mass, that Peter had just identified. Then he bestowed on Peter some very important privileges in that congregation. He did not give Peter primacy over the other apostles, as some have assumed, but he gave him responsibilities. He gave Peter "the keys of the kingdom." (Matt. 16:19) It would be Peter's privilege to open the hope of entering God's Kingdom to three different fields of mankind—first to the Jews, then to the Samaritans, and finally to the Gentiles, or non-Jews.

15 However, Jesus later stated that those given much would have more to answer for, and the truth of those words is borne out in Peter's case. (Luke 12:48) Jesus continued to reveal vital truths about the Messiah, including the certainty of his own impending suffering and death at Jerusalem. Peter was disturbed to hear such things. He took Jesus aside and rebuked him, saying:

---

14. Jesus bestowed on Peter what important privileges?
15. What led Peter to rebuke Jesus, and in what words?

"Be kind to yourself, Lord; you will not have this destiny at all."
—Matt. 16:21, 22.

16 Peter surely meant well, so Jesus' reply must have come as a surprise. He turned his back on Peter, looked at the rest of the disciples—who had likely been thinking something similar—and said: "Get behind me, Satan! You are a stumbling block to me, because you think, not God's thoughts, but those of men." (Matt. 16:23; Mark 8:32, 33) Jesus' words contain practical counsel for us all. It is only too easy to allow human thinking to take priority over godly thinking. If we do so, even when we mean to help, we may inadvertently become proponents of Satan's purpose rather than God's. How, though, did Peter respond?

Only if we humbly accept discipline and learn from it can we continue to grow closer to Jesus Christ and his Father, Jehovah God

17 Peter must have realized that Jesus was not calling him Satan the Devil in any literal sense. After all, Jesus did not speak to Peter as he had to Satan. To Satan, Jesus had said: "Go away"; to Peter, he said: "Get behind me." (Matt. 4:10) Jesus did not cast off this apostle in whom he saw a great deal of good, but he simply corrected Peter's wrong thinking in this matter. It is not hard to see that Peter needed to stop getting in front of his Master as a stumbling block and needed to get back behind him as a supportive follower.

18 Did Peter argue, get angry, or sulk? No; he humbly accepted correction. He thus demonstrated loyalty again. All those who follow Christ will need correction at times. Only if we humbly accept discipline and learn from it can we continue to grow closer to Jesus Christ and his Father, Jehovah God.—*Read Proverbs 4:13.*

Loyalty Rewarded

19 Jesus soon made another startling statement: "Truly I say to you that there are some of those standing here that will not

16. How did Jesus correct Peter, and what practical counsel may all of us find in Jesus' words?
17. What did Jesus mean by telling Peter to "get behind" him?
18. How did Peter demonstrate loyalty, and how can we imitate him?
19. Jesus made what startling statement, and what may Peter have wondered?

Peter proved loyal even when he had to be corrected

taste death at all until first they see the Son of man coming in his kingdom." (Matt. 16:28) No doubt those words filled Peter with curiosity. What could Jesus possibly mean? Perhaps Peter wondered if the strong correction he had just received meant that no such special privileges would be coming his way.

20 About a week later, however, Jesus took James, John, and Peter up into "a lofty mountain"—perhaps Mount Hermon, which was not many miles distant. It was likely nighttime, since the three men were combating sleepiness. But as Jesus prayed, something happened that drove away any drowsiness.—Matt. 17:1; Luke 9:28, 29, 32.

21 Jesus began to change before their eyes. His face started to shine, to glow, until it became as brilliant as the sun. His

---

20, 21. (a) Describe the vision that Peter witnessed. (b) How did the conversation among the figures in the vision help to correct Peter?

clothes too were glistening white. Then two figures appeared with Jesus, one representing Moses and the other, Elijah. They conversed with him about "his departure that he was destined to fulfill at Jerusalem"—evidently his death and resurrection. How clear it was that Peter had been wrong to deny that Jesus had such a painful experience ahead of him!—Luke 9: 30, 31.

²² Peter felt compelled to participate somehow in this extraordinary vision—and perhaps to prolong it. It looked as if Moses and Elijah were parting from Jesus. So Peter spoke up: "Instructor, it is fine for us to be here, so let us erect three tents, one for you and one for Moses and one for Elijah." Of course, these visionary representations of two of Jehovah's long-dead servants did not need tents. Peter really did not know what he was saying. Are you not drawn to the man, though, for his enthusiastic and warm spirit?—Luke 9:33.

²³ Peter, James, and John received another reward that night. A cloud formed and loomed over them on the mountain. From it came a voice—the voice of Jehovah God! He said: "This is my Son, the one that has been chosen. Listen to him." Then the vision was over, and they were alone with Jesus on the mountain. —Luke 9:34-36.

²⁴ What a gift that transfiguration vision was for Peter—and for us! Decades later he wrote of the privilege he had that night of actually seeing a preview of Jesus as a glorious heavenly King and of being one of the "eyewitnesses of his magnificence." That vision confirmed many prophecies of God's Word and strengthened Peter's faith for the trials he had yet to face. (*Read 2 Peter 1:16-19.*) It can do the same for us if, like Peter, we remain loyal to the Master whom Jehovah has appointed over us, learning from him, accepting his discipline and correction, and humbly following him day by day.

TO THINK ABOUT . . .

- How did Peter's faith move him to be loyal when many abandoned Jesus?
- How did Peter's faith and loyalty help him to accept correction?
- How did the transfiguration vision strengthen Peter's faith?
- In what further ways would you like to imitate Peter's faith?

22, 23. (a) How did Peter show an enthusiastic and warm spirit? (b) Peter, James, and John received what other reward that night?

24. (a) How did the transfiguration vision benefit Peter? (b) How may we today benefit from the transfiguration vision?

Along with James and John, Peter was rewarded with a thrilling vision

CHAPTER TWENTY-THREE

He Learned Forgiveness From the Master

PETER would never forget that terrible moment when their eyes met. Did he see in Jesus' gaze some hint of disappointment or reproach? We cannot venture so far; the inspired record says only that "the Lord turned and looked upon Peter." (Luke 22: 61) But in that one glance, Peter saw the depth of his own failure. He realized that he had just done the very thing that Jesus had foretold, the one thing that Peter had insisted he would never do—he had disowned his beloved Master. It was a low point for Peter, perhaps the worst moment of the worst day of his life.

² All was not lost, though. Because Peter was a man of great faith, he still had an opportunity to recover from his mistakes and to learn one of Jesus' greatest lessons. It had to do with forgiveness. Each of us needs to learn the same lesson, so let us follow Peter on this difficult journey.

A Man With Much to Learn

³ About six months earlier in his hometown of Capernaum, Peter approached Jesus and asked: "Lord, how many times is my brother to sin against me and am I to forgive him? Up to seven times?" Peter likely thought that he was being generous. After all, the religious leaders of the day taught that one had to forgive only three times! Jesus replied: "Not, Up to seven times, but, Up to seventy-seven times."—Matt. 18:21, 22.

⁴ Was Jesus suggesting that Peter keep a running tally of a transgressor's actions? No; rather, by turning Peter's 7 into a 77, he was saying that love does not allow us to set an arbitrary limit on forgiveness. (1 Cor. 13:4, 5) Jesus showed that Peter had

---

1. What may have been the worst moment of Peter's life?

2. Peter needed to learn what lesson, and how may we benefit from his story?

3, 4. (a) What question did Peter ask Jesus, and what might Peter have thought? (b) How did Jesus show that Peter had been influenced by the spirit prevalent in those days?

"The Lord turned and looked upon Peter"

been influenced by a hard-hearted and unforgiving spirit that was prevalent in those days, one that meted out forgiveness as if by an accountant's ledger. However, divine forgiveness is expansive, generous.—*Read 1 John 1:7-9.*

⁵ Peter did not argue with Jesus. But did Jesus' lesson really reach his heart? Sometimes we learn the most about forgiveness when we realize how desperately we need it ourselves. So let us return to the events leading up to Jesus' death. In those difficult hours, Peter gave his Master many things to forgive.

A Growing Need for Forgiveness

⁶ It was a momentous evening—the final night of Jesus' earthly life. Jesus still had much to teach his apostles—for instance, about humility. Jesus set an example by humbly washing their feet, a job normally assigned to the lowliest of servants. At first, Peter questioned Jesus' actions. Then he refused the service. Next he insisted that Jesus wash not only his feet but also his hands and head! Jesus did not lose his patience but calmly explained the importance and meaning of what he was doing. —John 13:1-17.

⁷ Shortly thereafter, Peter further tested Jesus' patience. The apostles fell to bickering over who of them was the greatest, and Peter surely played a part in that shameful display of human pride. Nonetheless, Jesus corrected them kindly and even commended them for what they had done well; they had shown faithfulness in sticking to their Master. He foretold, however, that they would all abandon him. Peter countered that he would stick with Jesus even in the face of death. Jesus prophesied that, on the contrary, Peter would deny his Master three times that very night before a cock crowed twice. Peter then not only contradicted Jesus but boasted that he would prove more faithful than all the other apostles!—Matt. 26:31-35; Mark 14:27-31; Luke 22:24-28; John 13:36-38.

⁸ Was Jesus close to losing his patience with Peter? In fact, throughout this difficult time, Jesus kept looking for the good in his imperfect apostles. He knew that Peter would fail him, yet He said: "I have made supplication for you that your faith may

5. When might we learn the most about forgiveness?

6. How did Peter respond as Jesus tried to teach the apostles about humility, yet how did Jesus treat him?

7, 8. (a) In what ways did Peter further test Jesus' patience? (b) How did Jesus continue to show a kind, forgiving spirit?

not give out; and you, when once you have returned, strengthen your brothers." (Luke 22:32) Jesus thus expressed confidence in Peter's spiritual recovery and his return to faithful service. What a kind, forgiving spirit!

⁹ Later, in the garden of Gethsemane, Peter needed correction more than once. Jesus asked him, as well as James and John, to keep on the watch while He prayed. Jesus was in emotional agony and in need of support, but Peter and the others fell asleep repeatedly. Jesus made this empathetic and forgiving observation: "The spirit, of course, is eager, but the flesh is weak."—Mark 14:32-41.

¹⁰ Before long, a mob arrived, bearing torches and armed with swords and clubs. Here was a time to act with caution and discretion. Yet, Peter rashly leaped into action, swinging a sword at the head of Malchus, a slave of the high priest, and lopping off one of the man's ears. Jesus calmly corrected Peter, healed the wound, and explained a principle of nonviolence that guides His followers to this day. (Matt. 26:47-55; Luke 22:47-51; John 18:10, 11) Peter had already given his Master much to forgive. His case may remind us that we all sin frequently. (**Read James 3:2.**) Who of us does not need divine forgiveness every single day? For Peter, though, the night was far from over. The worst lay ahead.

Peter's Worst Failure

¹¹ Jesus reasoned with the mob that if they were looking for him, they should let his apostles go. Peter watched helplessly as the mob bound Jesus. Then Peter fled, as did his fellow apostles.

¹² Peter and John stopped in their flight, perhaps near the house of the former High Priest Annas, where Jesus was first taken for questioning. As Jesus was led from there, Peter and John followed but "at a good distance." (Matt. 26:58; John 18:12, 13) Peter was no coward. It surely took a measure of courage to follow at all. The mob was armed, and Peter had already wounded one of them. Still, we do not here see in Peter's example the kind of loyal love that he himself had professed—a willingness to die by his Master's side if need be.—Mark 14:31.

_____

9, 10. (a) In the garden of Gethsemane, what correction did Peter need? (b) Peter's case may remind us of what?

11, 12. (a) How did Peter show a measure of courage after Jesus' arrest? (b) In what way did Peter's example fall short of what he himself had professed?

[13] Like Peter, many today seek to follow Christ "at a good distance"—in such a way that no one else will notice. But as Peter himself later wrote, the only way to follow Christ properly is to stick as close to Him as we can, imitating His example in all things, regardless of the consequences.—*Read 1 Peter 2:21.*

[14] Peter's cautious steps finally brought him up to the gate of one of Jerusalem's most imposing mansions. It was the home of Caiaphas, the wealthy and powerful high priest. Such homes were usually built around a courtyard, with a gate in the front. Peter reached the gate and was refused entrance. John, who knew the high priest and was already inside, came and got the door-keeper to admit Peter. It seems that Peter did not stick close to John; nor did he try to get inside the house to stand at his Master's side. He stayed in the courtyard, where some slaves and servants were passing the chilly night hours in front of a bright fire, watching as the false witnesses against Jesus paraded in and out of the trial going on inside.—Mark 14:54-57; John 18:15, 16, 18.

[15] In the firelight, the girl who had admitted Peter at the gate was able to see him better. She recognized him. She said accusingly: "You, too, were with Jesus the Galilean!" Caught off guard, Peter denied knowing Jesus—or even understanding what the girl was talking about. He went to stand near the gatehouse, trying to be inconspicuous, but another girl noticed him and pointed out the same fact: "This man was with Jesus the Nazarene." Peter swore: "I do not know the man!" (Matt. 26:69-72; Mark 14:66-68) Perhaps it was after this second denial that Peter heard a cock crowing, but he was too distracted to be reminded of the prophecy Jesus had uttered just hours earlier.

[16] A little while later, Peter was still trying desperately to escape notice. But a group of people standing around in the courtyard approached. One of them was related to Malchus, the slave whom Peter had wounded. He said to Peter: "I saw you in the garden with him, did I not?" Peter felt driven to convince them that they were wrong. So he swore to the matter, evidently saying that a curse should come upon him if he was lying. That was Peter's third denial. No sooner were the words out of his mouth than a cock crowed—the second one Peter heard that night. —John 18:26, 27; Mark 14:71, 72.

---

13. What is the only way to follow Christ properly?

14. How did Peter pass the nighttime hours during Jesus' trial?

15, 16. Explain how Jesus' prophecy about three denials was fulfilled.

¹⁷ Jesus had just come out onto a balcony overlooking the courtyard. In that moment, described at the outset of this chapter, his eyes met Peter's. It dawned on Peter just how terribly he had failed his Master. Peter left the courtyard, crushed by the weight of his own guilt. He headed into the streets of the city, his way lit by the sinking full moon. The tears welled up. The sights swam before his eyes. He broke down and wept bitterly.—Mark 14:72; Luke 22:61, 62.

¹⁸ In the wake of such a failure, it is all too easy for a person to assume that his sin is too terrible for forgiveness to be possible. Peter may have wondered as much himself. Was it so?

Peter gave his Master much to forgive, but who of us does not need forgiveness every day?

Was Peter Beyond Forgiveness?

¹⁹ It is hard to imagine the depth of Peter's pain as the morning broke and the events of the day unfolded. How he must have reproved himself when Jesus died later that day after hours of torment! Peter must have shuddered to think of how he had added to his Master's pain on what turned out to be the last day of His life as a man. Deep though the abyss of his sadness surely was, Peter did not give in to despair. We know as much because we soon find him in association with his spiritual brothers again. (Luke 24:33) No doubt all the apostles regretted how they had behaved on that dark night, and they brought one another a measure of comfort.

²⁰ In a way, we here see Peter in one of his finer moments. When a servant of God falls, what matters most is not the depth of his fall but the strength of his determination to get up again, to set matters right. (**Read Proverbs 24:16.**) Peter showed genuine faith by gathering with his brothers despite his low spirits. When one is burdened by sadness or regret, isolation is tempting but dangerous. (Prov. 18:1) The wise course is to stay close to fellow believers and regain spiritual strength.—Heb. 10:24, 25.

17, 18. (a) How did Peter react when it dawned on him how terribly he had failed his Master? (b) What may Peter have wondered?

19. How must Peter have felt about his failure, yet how do we know that he did not give in to despair?

20. What can we learn from Peter's actions in one of his finer moments?

21 Because he was with his spiritual brothers, Peter got to hear the shocking news that Jesus' body was not in the tomb. Peter and John ran to the tomb where Jesus had been buried and the entrance had been sealed. John, likely a younger man, arrived first. Finding the entrance of the tomb open, he hesitated. Not Peter. Though he was winded, he went straight in. It was empty!—John 20:3-9.

22 Did Peter believe that Jesus had been resurrected? Not at first, even though faithful women reported that angels had appeared to them to announce that Jesus had risen from the dead. (Luke 23:55–24:11) But by the end of that day, all traces of sadness and doubt in Peter's heart had melted away. Jesus lived, now a mighty spirit! He appeared to all his apostles. He did something else first, though, something private. The apostles said that day: "For a fact the Lord was raised up and he appeared to Simon!" (Luke 24:34) Similarly, the apostle Paul later wrote about that remarkable day when Jesus "appeared to Cephas, then to the twelve." (1 Cor. 15:5) Cephas and Simon are other names for Peter. Jesus appeared to him that day—evidently when Peter was alone.

23 The details of that touching reunion are left unrecorded in the Bible. They remain between Jesus and Peter. We can only imagine how moved Peter was to see his beloved Lord alive again and to have an opportunity to express his sorrow and repentance. More than anything in the world, Peter wanted forgiveness. Who can doubt that Jesus extended it, and in abundance at that? Christians today who fall into sin need to remember Peter's case. Never should we assume that we are beyond the reach of divine forgiveness. Jesus perfectly reflects his Father, who "will forgive in a large way."—Isa. 55:7.

Further Proof of Forgiveness

24 Jesus told his apostles to go to Galilee, where they would meet him again. When they arrived, Peter decided to go out fishing on the Sea of Galilee. Several others accompanied him. Once

21. Because he had gathered with his spiritual brothers, what news did Peter hear?
22. What caused all traces of sadness and doubt in Peter's heart to melt away?
23. Why do Christians today who fall into sin need to remember Peter's case?
24, 25. (a) Describe Peter's night of fishing on the Sea of Galilee. (b) What was Peter's reaction to Jesus' miracle the next morning?

again, Peter found himself on the lake where he had spent much of his earlier life. The creaking of the boat, the lapping of the waves, the feel of the coarse nets in his hands must all have seemed comfortingly familiar. The men caught no fish all that night.—Matt. 26:32; John 21:1-3.

25 At dawn, though, a figure called from the shore and urged the fishermen to cast their nets on the other side of the boat. They complied and pulled in a great catch of 153 fish! Peter knew who that person was. He leaped from the boat and swam

Peter leaped from the boat and swam ashore

203

ashore. On the beach, Jesus gave his faithful friends a meal of fish cooked over charcoal. He focused on Peter.—John 21:4-14.

²⁶ Jesus asked Peter if he loved his Lord "more than these" —evidently pointing to the large haul of fish. In Peter's heart, would love for the fishing business compete with love for Jesus? Just as Peter had denied his Lord three times, Jesus now gave him the opportunity to affirm his love three times before his fellows. As Peter did so, Jesus told him how to show that love: by putting sacred service ahead of all else, feeding, strengthening, and shepherding Christ's flock, His faithful followers.—Luke 22: 32; John 21:15-17.

²⁷ Jesus thus confirmed that Peter was still useful to him and to his Father. Peter would play a valuable role in the congregation under Christ's direction. What powerful proof of Jesus' full forgiveness! Surely that mercy touched Peter, and he took it to heart.

²⁸ Peter faithfully carried out his assignment for many years. He strengthened his brothers, as Jesus had commanded on the eve of His death. Peter worked kindly and patiently at shepherding and feeding Christ's followers. The man called Simon came to live up to the name that Jesus had given him—Peter, or Rock—by becoming a steady, strong, reliable force for good in the congregation. Much evidence to that effect is found in the two warm, personal letters Peter wrote that became valuable books of the Bible. Those letters show, too, that Peter never forgot the lesson he had learned from Jesus about forgiveness.—*Read 1 Peter 3:8, 9; 4:8.*

²⁹ May we learn that lesson as well. Do we daily ask God's forgiveness for our many errors? Do we then accept that forgiveness and believe in its power to cleanse us? And do we extend forgiveness to those around us? If we do, we will imitate the faith of Peter—and the mercy of his Master.

TO THINK ABOUT . . .

- How did Peter display a faulty view of forgiveness?
- In what ways did Peter test Jesus' forgiveness?
- How did Jesus show forgiveness toward Peter?
- In what ways would you like to imitate Peter's faith and Jesus' mercy?

26, 27. (a) What opportunity did Jesus give Peter three times? (b) Jesus provided what proof of his full forgiveness of Peter?
28. How did Peter come to live up to his name?
29. How can we imitate the faith of Peter and the mercy of his Master?

Conclusion

"Be imitators of those who through faith and patience inherit the promises."
—HEBREWS 6:12.

FAITH. It is a beautiful word, one that names a very appealing quality. However, when we come across that word, we would do well to think of another one: "Urgent!" After all, if we do not have faith, we urgently need to acquire it. And if we do have faith, we urgently need to protect and nourish it. Why?

² Imagine that you are traversing a vast desert. You are in critical need of water. When you find some, you have to protect it from the sun. Then you need to be able to replenish your supply so that it will last you until you arrive at your destination. Today, we all live in a spiritual desert, a world where genuine faith—like that water—is rare and tends to evaporate quickly unless it is protected and replenished. Our need is pressing; just as we cannot live without water, we cannot survive spiritually without faith.—Rom. 1:17.

³ Jehovah knows how urgently we need faith, and he knows how hard it is to build and maintain faith today. No doubt, that is why he has provided examples for us to imitate. Jehovah inspired the apostle Paul to write: "Be imitators of those who through faith and patience inherit the promises." (Heb. 6:12) And that is why Jehovah's organization has encouraged us to work hard to imitate the examples of faithful men and women, such as those we have considered in these pages. What, though, should we do now? Let us remember two things: (1) We need to keep strengthening our faith; (2) we need to keep our hope clearly in mind.

⁴ *Keep strengthening your faith.* Faith has a great enemy—Satan. The ruler of the world has turned this system of things into a kind of desert that is hostile to faith. He is far stronger than we are. Should we despair of developing and strengthening our faith? Never! Jehovah is the great Friend of all who seek genuine faith. He assures us that with Him on our side, we can oppose the Devil and even send him fleeing from us! (Jas. 4:7) We oppose him by taking time each day to strengthen our faith and build it up. How?

1, 2. Why is it vital that we build faith now? Illustrate.

3. What has Jehovah provided to help us build faith, and what are two things that we need to remember to do?

4. How has Satan proved to be an enemy of faith, yet why should we not despair?

⁵ As we have seen, the Bible's men and women of faith were not born faithful. They became living proof that faith is a product of Jehovah's holy spirit. (Gal. 5:22, 23) They prayed for help, and Jehovah kept strengthening their faith as a result. Let us do as they did, never forgetting that Jehovah gives his spirit generously to those who ask for it and who work in harmony with their prayers. (Luke 11:13) Is there more that we can do?

⁶ In this book, we have discussed only a few examples of outstanding faith. There are many, many others! (*Read Hebrews 11:32.*) Each one—in its own way—offers a rich field for prayerful, heartfelt study. If we merely rush through Bible accounts about people of faith, we will not firmly establish our own faith. To benefit fully from our reading, we need to spend time digging into the context and the background of Bible accounts. If we always remember that those imperfect men and women had "feelings like ours," their examples will become more real to us. (Jas. 5:17) With empathy, we can imagine how they might have felt as they faced challenges and problems similar to our own.

⁷ We also fortify our faith through our actions. After all, "faith without works is dead." (Jas. 2:26) Just imagine how the men and women we have discussed would rejoice if they were assigned to do the kind of work that Jehovah has asked us to do today!

⁸ For example, what if Abraham had been told that he could worship Jehovah, not at crude altars of stone erected in the wilderness, but among organized groups of fellow worshippers in pleasant Kingdom Halls and at large conventions, where the promises that he saw only "afar off" are discussed and explained in glorious detail? (*Read Hebrews 11:13.*) And what if Elijah had been told that his work involved, not executing wicked Baal prophets while he was trying to serve Jehovah under the rule of a wicked apostate king, but peacefully visiting people to deliver a message of comfort and hope? Really, would not the Bible's men and women of faith have jumped at the chance to worship Jehovah as we do today?

⁹ So let us keep strengthening our faith by actions. As we do so, we will be making practical application of the examples of men and women of faith found in God's inspired

---

5. How did the Bible's faithful men and women acquire their faith? Explain.

6. How can we gain the most benefit from our study of Bible accounts?

7-9. (a) How might some of the men and women of faith in Bible times have felt about worshipping Jehovah in the way that we do today? (b) Why should we strengthen our faith by actions?

Word. As mentioned in the Introduction, we will come to feel ever closer to them as friends. However, such friendships may soon become far more substantial.

¹⁰ *Keep your hope clearly in mind.* Faithful men and women have always drawn strength from their God-given hope. Do you? For example, imagine the joy of meeting faithful servants of God as they return to life in the "resurrection of . . . the righteous." (**Read Acts 24:15.**) What are some questions that you would like to ask them?

¹¹ When you meet Abel, will you be eager to ask him what his parents were like? Or you might ask: "Did you ever speak to those cherubs guarding the way to Eden? Did they answer?" What about Noah? You might ask him: "Were you ever frightened of the Nephilim? How did you care for all those animals during that year in the ark?" If you meet Abraham, you might ask: "Did you have any contact with Shem? Who taught you about Jehovah? Was it hard to leave Ur?"

¹² Likewise, consider some questions you might want to ask the faithful women who are resurrected. "Ruth, what moved you to become a worshipper of Jehovah?" "Abigail, were you afraid to tell Nabal about how you had helped David?" "Esther, what happened to you and Mordecai after the story in the Bible ended?"

¹³ Of course, those faithful men and women may be brimming with questions for you too. What a thrill to tell them about the climactic last days and how Jehovah blessed his people during hard times! No doubt they will be deeply moved to learn how Jehovah fulfilled all his promises. In those days to come, it will no longer be a challenge to make God's loyal servants in the Bible record come to life in our minds. They will be there with us, in Paradise! So keep doing everything you can now to make those people real to you. Keep imitating their faith. May you enjoy serving Jehovah along with them as your dear friends forever!

---

10. What joy will we have in Paradise?

11, 12. In the new world, what questions might you ask of (a) Abel? (b) Noah? (c) Abraham? (d) Ruth? (e) Abigail? (f) Esther?

---

13. (a) What kind of questions might resurrected ones have for you? (b) How do you feel about the prospect of meeting faithful men and women of ancient times?

SELECTED OFFICES OF JEHOVAH'S WITNESSES

AUSTRALIA: PO Box 280, Ingleburn, NSW 1890. **BELGIUM:** rue d'Argile-Potaardestraat 60, B-1950 Kraainem. **BENIN:** BP 312, AB-Calavi. **BRITAIN:** The Ridgeway, London NW7 1RN. **BURUNDI:** BP 2150, Bujumbura. **CANADA:** PO Box 4100, Georgetown, ON L7G 4Y4. **CONGO, DEMOCRATIC REPUBLIC OF:** BP 634, Limete, Kinshasa. **GEORGIA:** Postbox 237, Tbilisi, 0102. **GERMANY:** 65617 Selters. **ITALY:** Via della Bufalotta 1281, I-00138 Rome RM. **KENYA:** PO Box 21290, Nairobi 00505. **LIBERIA:** PO Box 10-0380, 1000 Monrovia 10. **NIGERIA:** PMB 1090, Benin City 300001, Edo State. **RWANDA:** BP 529, Kigali. **SCANDINAVIA:** PO Box 340, DK-4300 Holbæk. **SOUTH AFRICA:** Private Bag X2067, Krugersdorp, 1740. **UNITED STATES OF AMERICA:** 25 Columbia Heights, Brooklyn, NY 11201-2483. www.jw.org